Puppet Animals Tell Bible Stories

PUPPET ANIMALS TELL BIBLE STORIES

Marie M. Chapman

Cover and Illustrations by Caroline A. Cleaveland

ACCENT BOOKS
Denver, Colorado

ACCENT BOOKS

A division of Accent Publications, Inc.
12100 W. Sixth Avenue
P.O. Box 15337
Denver, Colorado 80215

Library of Congress Catalog Card Number 77-075134

ISBN 0-916406-74-1

First Printing 1977
Second Printing 1978
Third Printing 1979
Fourth Printing 1981
Fifth Printing 1983

Contents

Making the Puppets

Puppets fascinate children. And not children only. From time immemorial puppet shows have furnished dramatic entertainment, tragic or comic, to all kinds of audiences.

Puppet shows have conveyed political propaganda to adults. They are used with marked effect on television programs to delight millions with special skits and unusual commercials. Wherever they are used and whatever the purpose, eyes are glued in wonder to the sight of inanimate objects that move and "speak."

Puppets prove popular in Sunday Schools, too. In a department buzzing with whispers and shuffling feet, silence falls like a curtain when the puppets begin their action. No one wants to miss a trick.

But where can one obtain puppets? Busy leaders can buy many types of puppets ready-made, some fairly inexpensive. (A list of resources is provided at the back of the book which includes sources of ready-made puppets.) But handmade puppets, particularly animals, continue most readily to captivate pupils of all ages. With a few basic materials and a minimum of direction, even a novice can charm an audience as his animal puppets tell the Bible stories in this book.

You can transform a variety of ordinary materials into appealing puppets. Since certain animal shapes adapt more easily to one basic material than to another the puppets are grouped under the basic materials used to make them. You will find instructions for all the puppets used in the stories of this book under oatmeal box puppets, sack puppets or cloth puppets.

Probably every puppet in this collection could be made from a sack. However, you must bear in mind that the "worst teaching method" is the one that is used all the time. The more variety you have in the appearance of the puppets the more interest you will create.

Wherever glue is mentioned, Elmer's glue will serve well.

9

Oatmeal Box Puppets

Animal Puppets with Long Heads and Big Mouths

Donkey	Camel	Dog
Ox	Cow	Fox

For animals with long heads and big mouths, cut the oatmeal box exactly in half the long way. Cover the two openings which were made through the middle with two cardboard strips. Then cover these strips with red wool, felt or paper for the inside of the mouth. Hinge the two sections of the head together so that the mouth will open. See Sketches 1 and 2.

Cover the outside with material that simulates the animal's hide—plush, vinyl or colored paper. Glue or staple on additional material to the head to conceal the puppeteer's arm.

Sketch 1

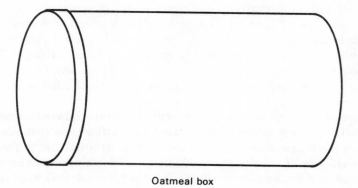

Oatmeal box

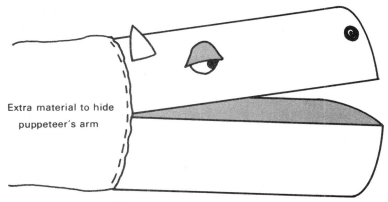

Round part of small oatmeal box cut in half the long way

Donkey, Ox, Camel, Cow, Dog, Fox

Animal Puppets with Wide Faces

Sheep	Lion	Tiger
Raven	Rabbit	

For animals with wide faces leave the oatmeal box whole and hold it upright. In this way the rounded part forms the animal's face. Remove the lid carefully and turn the box upside down. Fold the box lid in half so that the edges of the strips meet. This forms the mouth and the teeth. Use a marker to draw teeth around the rim of the lid. Attach the mouth, the top fold of the lid, with glue to the lower rim of the box. The hand will enter the other half of the open end and manipulate the mouth near the bottom; the eyes, ears, and other facial parts are exaggerated in the upper part of the round box. See Sketches 3 and 4. Cover the box with plush, velour, velvet or vinyl in a color natural for the animal. See the section "Facial and Other Features" for instructions in completing the puppets.

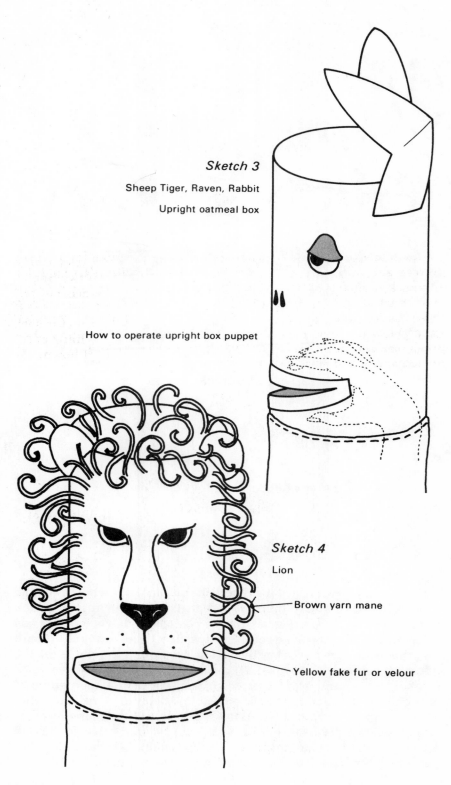

Sketch 3

Sheep Tiger, Raven, Rabbit

Upright oatmeal box

How to operate upright box puppet

Sketch 4

Lion

Brown yarn mane

Yellow fake fur or velour

12

Sack Puppets

Cat   Pig   Owl

The easiest puppets to improvise are those made from small grocery sacks. Each sack should be about the width of two hands. The sack when folded has a flap at the bottom. This flap becomes the main part of the head including the upper part of the mouth. See Sketches 5 and 6. The lower part of the mouth is placed on the sack itself below the folded flap. When the four fingers of the hand of the puppeteer are poked into the flap and moved up and down, the mouth opens and shuts.

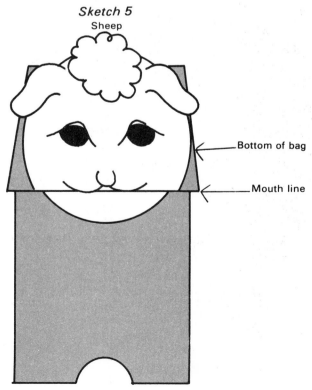

Sketch 5
Sheep

Bottom of bag

Mouth line

13

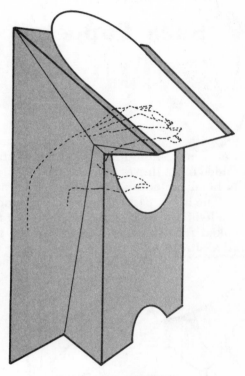

How to work sack puppet

You can easily construct from sacks the Eavesdropping Owl (Sketch 7), Porky, the Pig (Sketch 8), and Kitty, the Cat (Sketch 9).

Make elaborate sack puppets by gluing cloth to the sack or using simulated fur material for Kitty, the Cat.

If you can find a large size magazine picture of the front view of the face of the animal, this will add realism to the puppet. The head must be large enough so the mouth can be cut in half horizontally and mounted on the flap of the sack so that it can be opened and closed. Instead, you may sketch the following simple outlines on the sack and color them with a felt tipped marker. If you wish to build your puppet's face with glued-on features see the section "Facial and Other Features."

Sketch 7

Owl

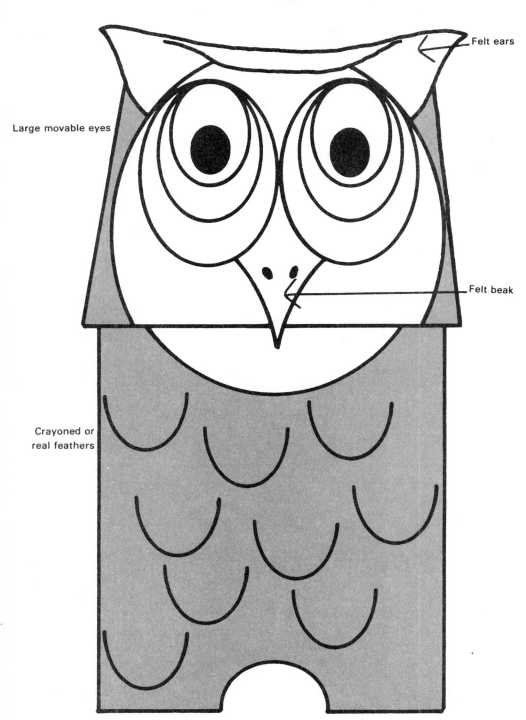

Large movable eyes

Felt ears

Felt beak

Crayoned or
real feathers

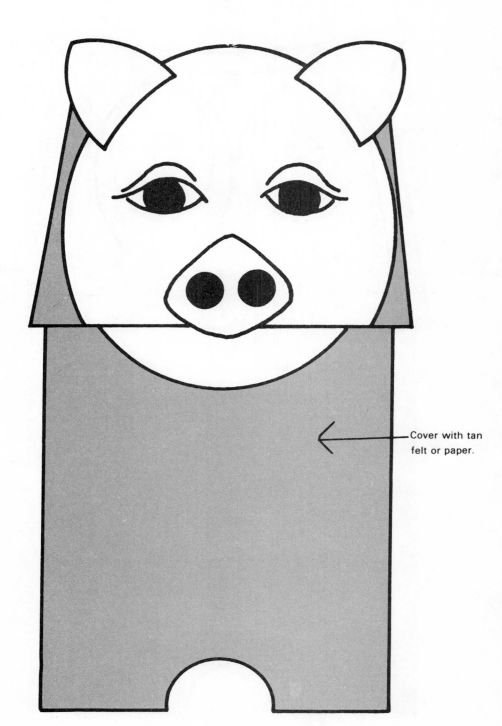

Cover with tan
felt or paper.

Sketch 9
Cat

Yarn whiskers
stiffened with glue

Fake fur

Cloth Puppets

Puppets Which Can Be Made from One Basic Pattern

Mouse   Cat   Whale
Rat   Rabbit

For the Mouse, Rat, Cat, Rabbit and Whale cut and sew material of a suitable color and texture for the animal so that your hand will slide into it easily. See Sketches 10, 11, and 12. Extend the material to cover a good part of your arm.

If you want to make one basic puppet do the work of several, make the basic shape given in the pattern. See Sketches 10, 11, 12, 13, 14, 15 and 16. Choose a color that would be suitable for several of the animals—for instance tan could be used for Mouse, Rat, Cat or Rabbit. Different features such as the eyes and ears may be attached temporarily. Use Velcro tape which is available in fabric sections of department stores or in fabric stores. Attach small pieces of this tape, which comes in tan or black, to the puppet where you want the ears and eyes. Make ears and eyes according to the patterns given. On the underside of each of them attach a small piece of this Velcro tape. Two pieces of this tape will adhere to each other but when the top piece is pulled it will come free of the other piece. This will enable you to produce several puppets by merely adding the appropriate eyes and ears to a basic puppet shape.

There are advantages to having separate puppets with permanent eyes and ears. Choose a different color for each puppet. A bluish gray or charcoal terrycloth would be nice for the Whale. Turn pieces of gray wool, velvet or short simulated fur into a Rat or Mouse. The Rat should be larger than the Mouse so the audience can distinguish between them. (A difference in size, however, is not too important since both Mouse and Rat do not appear in the same story.) If you like you could make the mouse brown and the rat gray.

After cutting the pattern for the top and for the under part of the body, fold the red felt for the lining of the mouth as shown in Sketch 11. Insert the folded piece between the top of the body and the underpart of the body. Sew the top part of the mouth lining to the top of the body, and the lower part of the mouth lining to the under part of the body. Put four fingers in the section between the top lining of the mouth and the top of the body just above it. Put your thumb

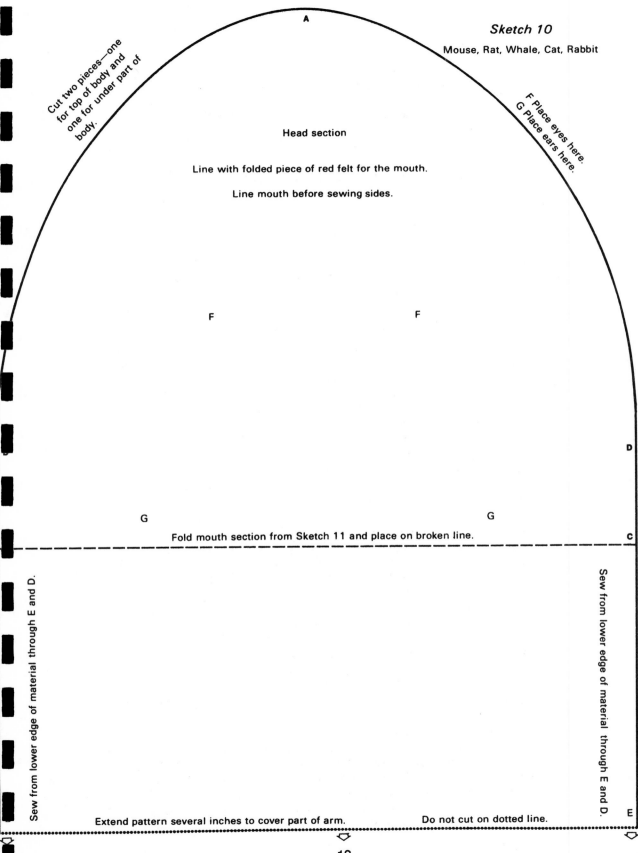

Cut two pieces—one for top of body and one for under part of body.

Sketch 10

Mouse, Rat, Whale, Cat, Rabbit

A

F Place eyes here.
G Place ears here.

Head section

Line with folded piece of red felt for the mouth.

Line mouth before sewing sides.

F   F

D

G   G

C

Fold mouth section from Sketch 11 and place on broken line.

Sew from lower edge of material through E and D.

Sew from lower edge of material through E and D.

Extend pattern several inches to cover part of arm.   Do not cut on dotted line.

E

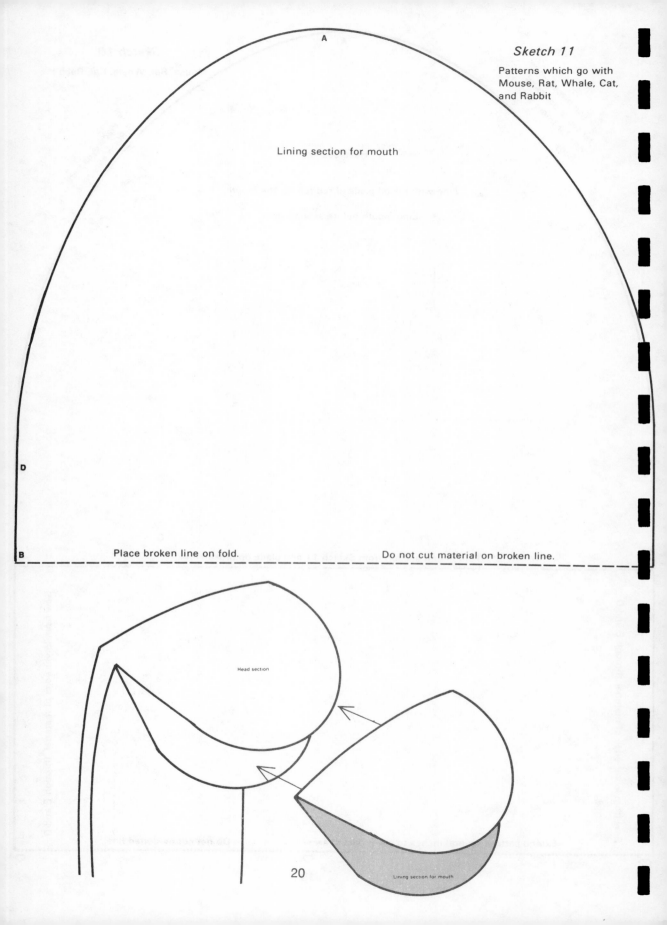

A

Patterns which go with
Mouse, Rat, Whale, Cat,
and Rabbit

Lining section for mouth

D

B Place broken line on fold.   Do not cut material on broken line.

Head section

Lining section for mouth

Sketch 12

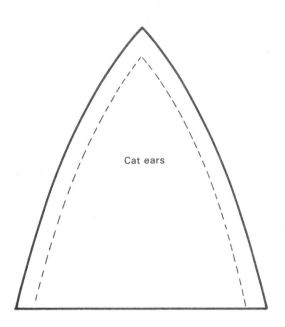

Cat ears

Sketch 13

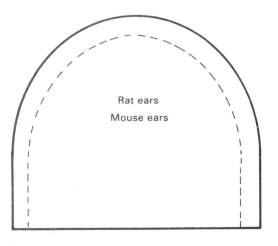

Rat ears
Mouse ears

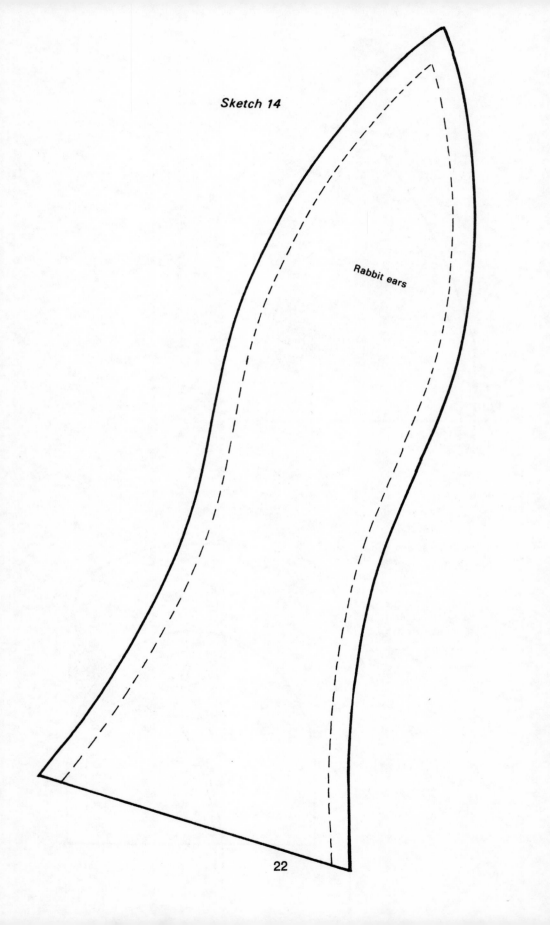

Sketch 14

Rabbit ears

22

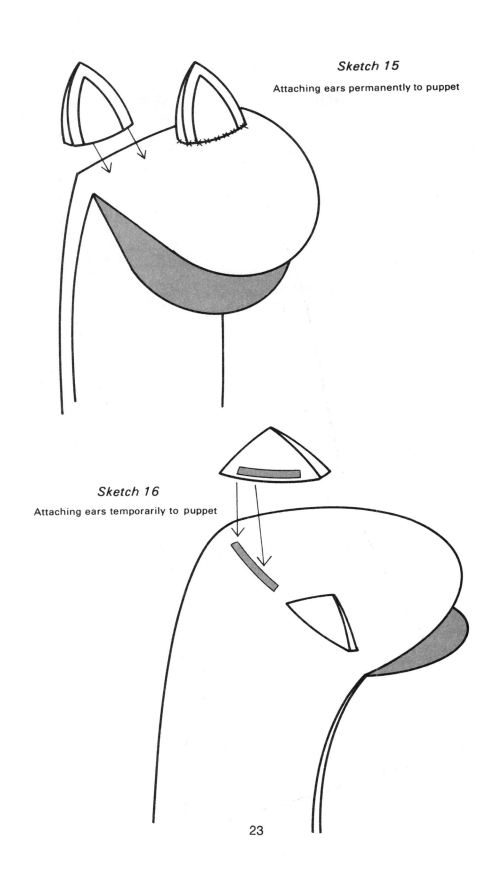

Sketch 15

Attaching ears permanently to puppet

Sketch 16

Attaching ears temporarily to puppet

23

between the lining of the mouth and the bottom of the body part underneath it. By moving those two parts the mouth opens and closes. If the head seems flimsy cut two pieces of cardboard slightly smaller than the mouth lining. Tape them together at the back of the throat so they will fold, and insert this cardboard in the space between the mouth lining and the upper and lower part of the head.

Instead of cutting a pattern for the Mouse you could use one finger of a glove. If you want a mouse family use as many fingers of the glove as you need. (You will need to cut up an old glove for this.) For the Mouse's features you may glue a tiny pompom on his nose and then give him three whiskers on each side. Run a thread through the area close to his nose and clip it off on both sides the length you want for the whiskers. You may use carpet thread which is fairly stiff or you may stiffen regular thread or string with a solution of one part Elmer's glue and one part water.

Use the same method of construction for the Rat's whiskers as for the Mouse.

Ears are distinguishing appendages for animal puppets. Cut the ears the shape shown on the pattern out of felt or the basic material from which the puppet is made. Add to the front of the ear a small piece of pink, peach or red material smaller than the ear. This shows the inside of the ear. A double thickness of the material for ears may make them stand up pertly, so will a number 12 or 14 wire around the inside edge of the ears. The wire is flexible enough so that if you want to bend the Rabbit's ears you may. With ears at different angles he can have a different "expression."

Also see the section "Facial and Other Features."

24

Frog Puppet

Make the frog puppet of bright green plush, velvet or terrycloth. See Sketches 17, 18, and 19 for the pattern. The main body of the frog pattern is in two pieces with another pattern for the mouth lining. Tape the patterns in Sketches 17 and 19 together before cutting from material. Place line CD on a fold of the green material. Cut two pieces like this—with the pattern placed on the fold both times. One of these forms the top of the body and the other forms the under part of the body.

Cut lining for the mouth area from red felt with the broken line EF on the fold. With this red piece folded join the top half of this mouth lining to the top head piece, and the bottom half of the lining to the bottom head piece so the fold of the mouth will come at the back of the throat.

After the mouth has been lined, sew around the edge of the body, but leave open from I to I. This is the opening for the hand which will control the puppet. Do not sew the mouth shut. Stuff each leg with one nylon stocking or the equivalent. Glue on large movable or felt eyes with Elmer's glue.

To operate this puppet put your fingers in the head section between mouth lining and the top of the head. Slip your thumb in the section below the mouth lining and the material of the under part of the mouth.

Stuffed Animal Puppets

Take out a part of the stuffing in children's stuffed animal toys, make an opening for the hand, bind it, and you will have a cute puppet.

Leave some of the stuffing in the head, arms and legs to give the puppet a nice shape. Prepare a place for your fingers in the head and arms. Secure the stuffing in those places to make sure it will not fall out.

Decide on the best place to make an opening to fit your hand. It would be wise to bind the opening with bias tape from a fabric store or to attach iron-on tape to prevent the opening from ravelling.

For these stuffed toys check out the toy counter at Goodwill, Salvation Army, thrift stores or garage sales. Clean soiled animals with Glamorene or Bissell's dry rug cleaner.

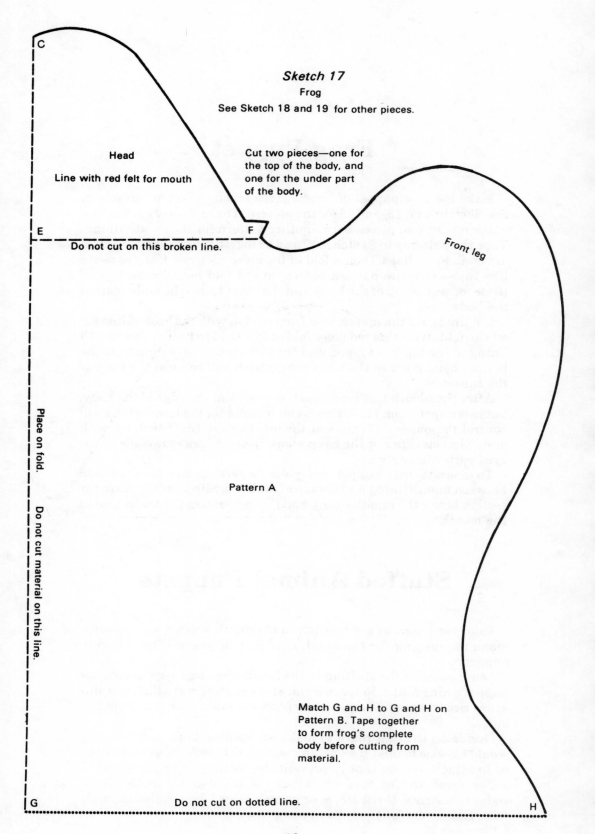

Sketch 17

Frog

See Sketch 18 and 19 for other pieces.

C

Head

Line with red felt for mouth

Cut two pieces—one for
the top of the body, and
one for the under part
of the body.

E   F

Do not cut on this broken line.

Front leg

Place on fold.   Do not cut material on this line.

Pattern A

Match G and H to G and H on
Pattern B. Tape together
to form frog's complete
body before cutting from
material.

G   Do not cut on dotted line.   H

Sketch 18

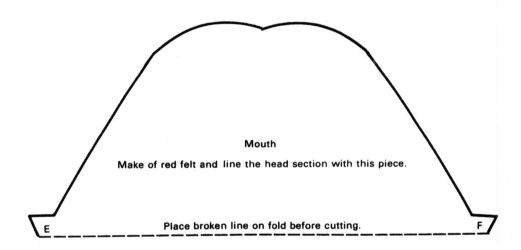

Mouth

Make of red felt and line the head section with this piece.

E — — — — — — — — Place broken line on fold before cutting. — — — — — — — F

Sketch 19

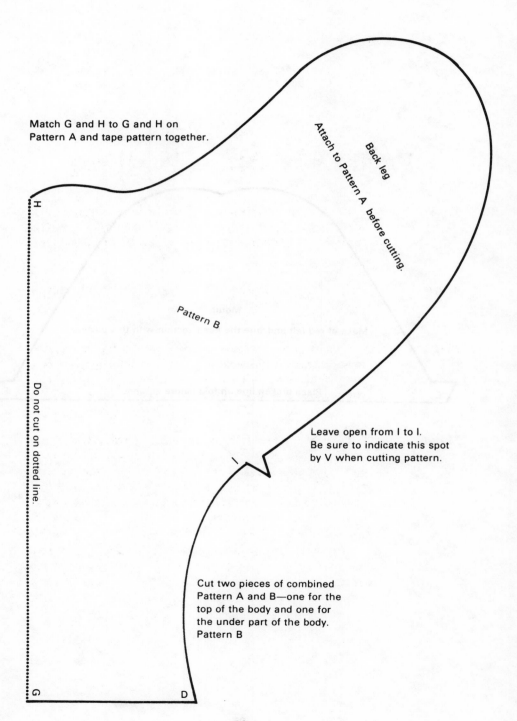

Match G and H to G and H on
Pattern A and tape pattern together.

Back leg

Attach to Pattern A before cutting.

H

Pattern B

Do not cut on dotted line.

Leave open from I to I.
Be sure to indicate this spot
by V when cutting pattern.

I

Cut two pieces of combined
Pattern A and B—one for the
top of the body and one for
the under part of the body.
Pattern B

G   D

Facial and Other Features

Eyes
For most puppets use for the eyes appropriate sized buttons, felt eyes, or movable eyes from a hobby store. Fasten them to the head with glue. See Sketch 20.

Nose
Glue on a felt nose or make two nostril dots with a felt marker or with paint.

Bird's bill
Raven gets a yellow pointed bill of felt or heavy construction paper. Round it by fastening the sides together loosely with masking tape. Glue the tape to the face, above the mouth. See Sketch 21.

Mane
Lion can use a yarn mane and beard. Attach one end of each piece of yarn to the body of the lion puppet with glue. Let the other end of the yarn hang free. When you move the lion in a puppet play his mane and beard can shake and move in a natural way.

Horns
Ox and Cow will look the part when they have curled construction paper horns. If you prefer make more realistic horns.

Sketch 20
Eyes

Eyes may be used on any style of puppet
Enlarge eyes to fit size of puppets used
Cut eyes from different colors of paper or felt

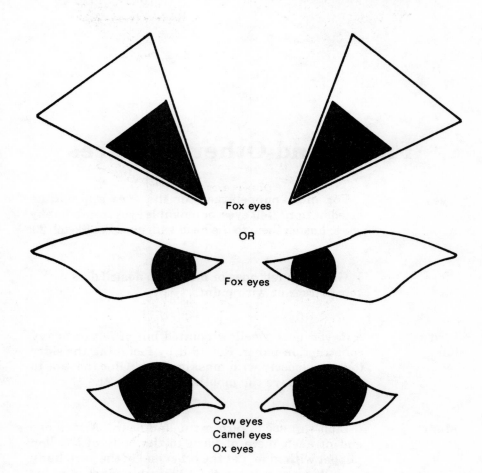

Fox eyes

OR

Fox eyes

Cow eyes
Camel eyes
Ox eyes

Eyelashes
Attach eyelashes behind eyes

Fold and attach

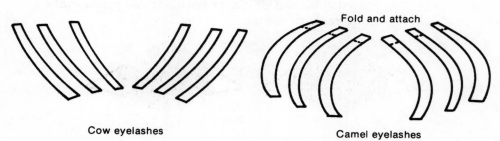

Cow eyelashes

Camel eyelashes

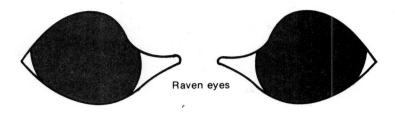
Raven eyes

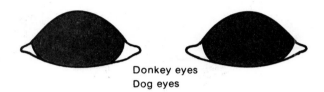
Donkey eyes
Dog eyes

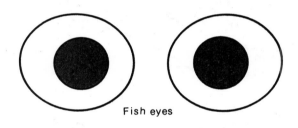
Fish eyes

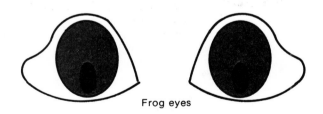
Frog eyes

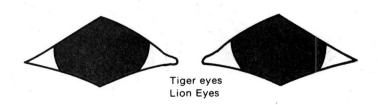
Tiger eyes
Lion Eyes

31

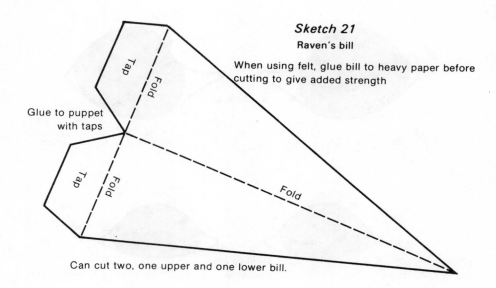

Sketch 21

Raven's bill

When using felt, glue bill to heavy paper before cutting to give added strength

Tap

Fold

Glue to puppet with taps

Tap

Fold

Fold

Can cut two, one upper and one lower bill.

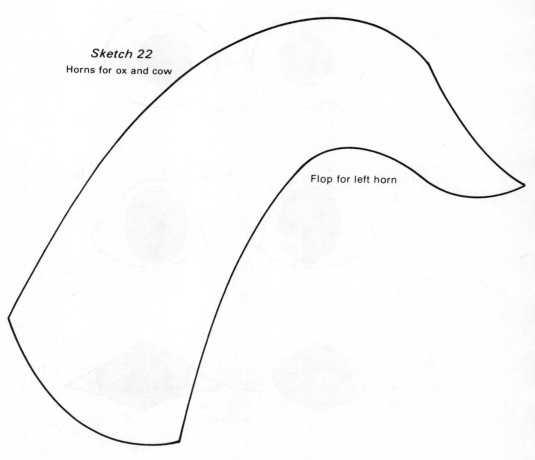

Sketch 22

Horns for ox and cow

Flop for left horn

Making a Puppet Stage

Using a few materials, some effort and a little imagination you can provide a puppet stage which will help make your stories come alive.

Stages may be made from different materials and in different ways ranging from simple to quite complex. A few of these are given below.

Large Box Stage

Puppeteer works from inside the box.

Boxes used to crate refrigerators, cabinets and large hardware items can be adapted to use for a stage. You may be able to obtain a suitable box from an appliance, hardware or building supply store.

A medium sized refrigerator box is quite suitable for even large audiences. It is also large enough for two puppeteers which makes it possible for you to use a larger variety of puppet plays.

The box should be sturdy and not too wide to get through the door of the building where it will be used. This type is quite satisfactory for using permanently in one place. It is more difficult to transport from place to place unless a pick-up truck or van is available. See Sketches 23, 24, and 25 for construction of this stage.

With a utility knife cut off the back of the box so the puppeteer can enter it. However, leave an inch of cardboard all the way around the edge so the box will be stronger. A box without a back on it or without a door will be more comfortable for the puppeteer. The inside of a box can sometimes be quite warm.

Cut away the top of the box leaving an inch of the cardboard all around for reinforcement. When you finish the box you want it to be

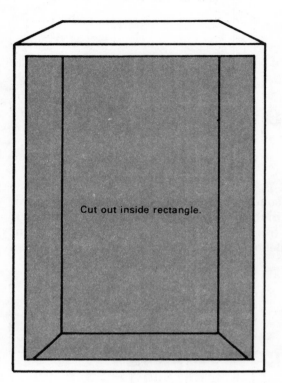

Sketch 23
Large Box Stage

Back of box stage

Cut out inside rectangle.

Sketch 24

Inside of large box stage
looking toward the front

Sketch 25

Side view of inside of large box stage

Puppeteer

Thin back curtains

Puppets

Curtains

Opening for audience to view puppets

Sketch 26

Completed large box stage

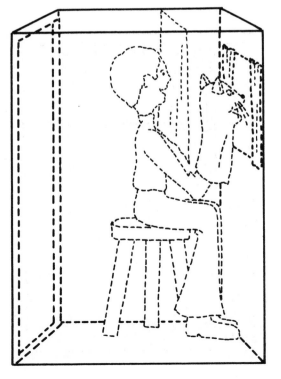

35

sturdy. It depends upon the construction of the box as to how much you can remove.

The box stages should have an opening cut out of the front of the box so the audience can see the puppets perform. Again leave a framework of the cardboard around the edges for reinforcement. Make the opening at least 6 to 12 inches high and about 18 inches wide. The measurements will depend upon the size of your box.

Cover all raw edges of your box with fairly wide masking tape. Paint, cover the box with contact paper, or use your imagination for original decorations.

Make curtains of opaque material which can be drawn together across the stage at certain times. A string drawn tightly on the inside of the box will hold them adequately. Puppets enter from the side behind these curtains.

Immediately behind the opening plan for enough room for the puppets to act out or tell their story. Behind the part of the stage which they will use hang another curtain. This should be thin enough so the puppeteer will be able to dimly see the audience.

For a view of the completed large box stage see Sketch 26.

Stage from Mover's Box

Puppeteer sits inside the wardrobe stage.

For a smaller and portable stage, use a clothes wardrobe such as moving companies provide, following the same general instructions above. This type of stage is collapsible and can be carried in the back of a standard sedan. It will accomodate only one puppeteer.

An Apron Box Stage

Puppeteer ties the Box Stage in front of him like an apron.

A stage made from a strong small box is easily portable and is more readily stored than the larger boxes. It is suitable for groups up to about 50. It can be made more quickly and easily than the other stages in this book. A box about 18 inches long and 12 inches high is quite satisfactory, but those exact measurements are not important. See Sketches 27, 28, 29, 30 and 31.

Cut off the two end pieces of the top of the box, B and C, and one side piece D. Raise piece A upright and fasten to it another heavy piece of cardboard to form the backdrop of the stage. See Sketch 28. Many cardboard boxes have another piece of cardboard in the bottom of the box to reinforce the box. This is just right for the extra piece if it is as heavy as the box material. Place it in front of lid A, and about two inches below the place where lid A connects to the box. This piece forms the backdrop for the puppets' action. Staple this extra piece, piece E, to piece A while held in the position described above. Use heavy building supply staples. You could probably get a builder or someone at the lumber yard to staple this for you.

The apron stage will be more comfortable for you if it fits you. Hold the box in front of you to help you determine the best places for the openings for the "sash." This can be made from sturdy material, cord or rope. See Sketch 29. Run the "sash" through the holes so that it is visible on the inside of the box. Then you can tie it around your waist. The stage will then hang in front of you.

Cut out the section marked on Sketch 29. This is the opening so your hands can manipulate the puppets. Leave at least an inch around the box edges so you will not weaken the box. Also leave at least two inches of the cardboard below and to the sides of the holes. This will be the area of greatest wear.

Bind all raw edges of the box with masking tape. Then spray paint it, or cover it with wallpaper, contact paper, or original designs.

Sketch 27

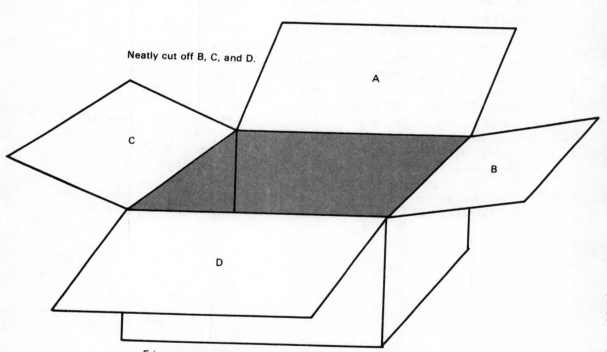

Neatly cut off B, C, and D.

A

C

B

D

E is a separate piece of sturdy cardboard.
It may come in bottom of box. It should
be the size of bottom of box.

Sketch 28

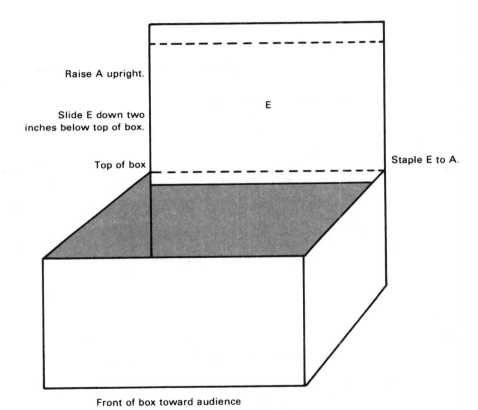

Raise A upright.

Slide E down two
inches below top of box.

E

Top of box

Staple E to A.

Front of box toward audience

Sketch 29

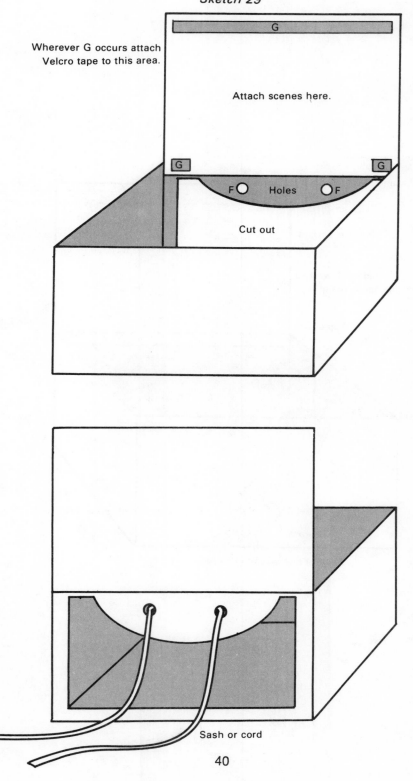

Wherever G occurs attach
Velcro tape to this area.

G

Attach scenes here.

G   G

F◯   Holes   ◯F

Cut out

Sash or cord

CLOSED

Puppet Animals Tell
Bible Stories

12/7/17

3.7 mil
11 from

14 $\frac{75}{}$ /G

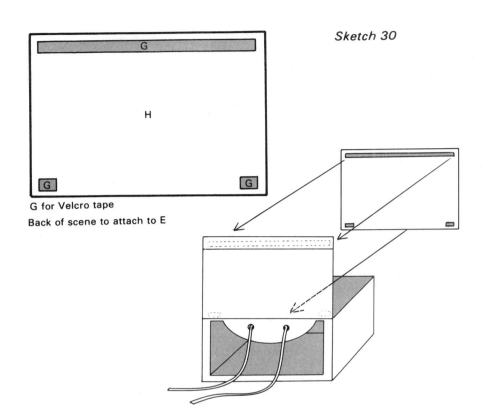

Sketch 30

G for Velcro tape

Back of scene to attach to E

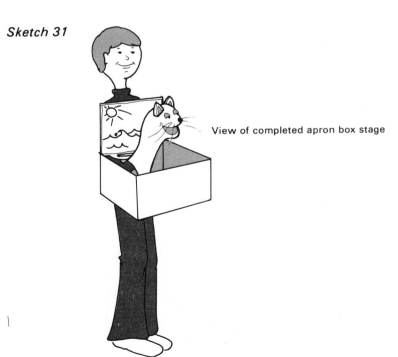

Sketch 31

View of completed apron box stage

A Table Box Stage

The puppeteer sits behind a table which supports the box stage.

Follow the directions for the apron box stage but eliminate the "sash." See Sketches 27, 28, 29, 30 and 31. Place the box stage on a table high enough so each one in the audience can see it easily. Work the puppets as you sit behind the box at the table.

A Hanging Puppet Stage

The puppeteer supports a hanging stage with a belt around his neck.

Use the same directions as for the apron box stage, only provide a belt to go around the neck instead of a sash.

Scenes for Puppet Stages

Using scenes—landscape, street, etc.—as a backdrop for your puppet plays will enhance this method of getting over Bible truth. However, it is not necessary. Good puppet productions can be given without suggesting the background.

The scenes given have been planned specifically for the apron, table and hanging box stages. However, they may be adapted easily to use with other stages.

Use very lightweight cardboard, tagboard or heavy shelf paper. First prepare this piece to adhere to the backdrop E in Sketch 28 following the directions below. Test it to be sure this material for your scene is not too heavy to adhere before you draw or paint it.

To hold the scenery piece to the backdrop so that it may be used for one story and changed for other stories use the special tape, Velcro tape. It is available in fabric stores.

Attach this tape across the back of each piece of scenery and also at the two lower corners. Also attach it to the backdrop E in these corresponding positions. When the scenery is pressed lightly to the backdrop the tape will hold it in place. See Sketches 29 and 30. Store the scenery in the bottom of the box stage. It should fit exactly.

Use the following scenes for the Bible stories: garden for garden of Eden, water scene for Noah, Jonah, and first part of Red Sea; field with road for Joseph, Balaam, Job, Samson, and David the shepherd boy; street for triumphal entry and Paul at Lystra; the jail or dungeon for Daniel and Paul and Silas; the rugged hill for Elijah, Gideon, David and Goliath, Samson and the crucifixion; bulrushes for baby Moses; the night scene for Nicodemus; and the pig pen for the prodigal son. See Sketches 32 through 40.

Sketch 32

Garden

The Garden of Eden

Sketch 33

Water with Waves

Noah and the Ark
Jonah
Crossing the Red Sea
Paul's Shipwreck

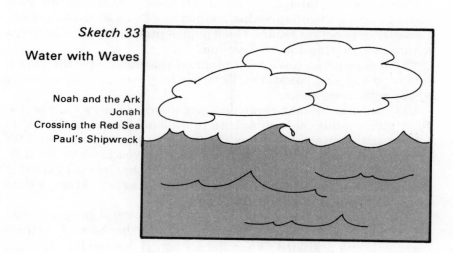

Sketch 34

Field and Road

Joseph Is Sold
Balaam
Job
Samson
David
the Shepherd Boy

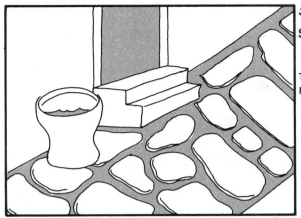

Sketch 35

Street

Triumphal Entry
Paul at Lystra

Sketch 36

Jail or Dungeon

Daniel in the Lions' Den
Paul and Silas

Sketch 37

Rugged Hill

Elijah and the Ravens
Gideon's Three Hundred
David and Goliath
Samson
The Crucifixion

Sketch 38

Bulrushes

The Baby in the Bulrushes

Sketch 39

Night Scene

Nicodemus

Sketch 40

Pig Pen

The Prodigal Son

Bible Stories Puppet Animals Tell

Kitty in the Garden

The Garden of Eden

You remember your mother, don't you? Well, I don't remember mine. You see, I never had a mother. Did somebody say, "That's silly—everybody has a mother"? But I won't keep you guessing. God made me, and my home was the Garden of Eden.

Some years later, I felt sorry for all the kittens born into the world. They had to worry about getting chased by dogs. Actually, in Eden one of my best friends was a big shaggy dog. All of us animals had such good times together. We wouldn't think of hurting each other. I even played hide-and-seek with the mouse and rat.

You've never seen a garden like the one where I lived. Think of the thickest, greenest grass you ever saw. That's what the green carpet of grass was like in Eden. Think of the brightest, prettiest flowers you've seen. They are nowhere nearly as beautiful as those in Eden. Think of the clearest, most sparkling river you ever waded into. The one I drank from in Eden was much clearer.

And there were no weeds in this beautiful garden. Not even one little weed. Everything was just right.

And I never had to wonder where my next meal was coming from. God planned for all of us animals to have enough to eat—even the elephants and giraffes and hippos. And then He gave us someone to look after us. He made a man.

47

This man, Adam, didn't have a pretty fur coat like I have. And he didn't use all four of his legs. The front legs just hung down at his sides. He couldn't run as fast as I can, and he couldn't jump as high as the kangaroo, and he wasn't nearly as big as the elephant. But still God made him king of the garden. He ruled all of us. One day, we all paraded past him and he gave us our names. My name is Cat but he calls me Kitty.

The next time I saw Adam, there was another one with him—just like him, only different. This other person was prettier. I found out she was a woman and her name was Eve. I purred when she patted my head and stroked my soft fur. I followed her around, hoping she would pat me some more. But there were so many of us animals to pat. I don't see why anyone would ever want to touch the tough skin of the hippo. It's not at all soft and fuzzy like mine.

One day I was running circles around a tree, trying to get a closer look at a bright orange creature that sat on a flower and then moved through the air to another flower. Adam and Eve were walking with God near that tree. I heard God say, "You can have the fruit of all the trees for food—except the fruit of this tree right here. If you eat that, you will die." I didn't know what "die" was, but the way God said it, I was sure I wouldn't eat any of that fruit.

Not long after that, I trotted along close to Eve. She was out for a walk looking at flowers and the animals. She stopped for awhile by the river and admired it. Then we came to the tree—God had said not to eat the fruit of that tree. A beautiful Snake was close to the tree. He was shiny, tall and very slim, weaving back and forth as he moved gracefully along.

The Snake said to Eve, "Hello. I was waiting to talk to you. I wanted to ask you this. Did God say you couldn't eat the fruit of every tree in the garden?"

Eve told him, "God said we could have everything we wanted, except the fruit of this tree right here. We can't eat it or even touch it, or we will die."

The Snake chuckled. "You won't die," he said. "God just knows that if you eat this fruit you will be like Him. You will know what is good and what is bad."

Eve looked at the bright-colored fruit. She reached out and touched one fruit gently. She pulled on it and it came off in her hand. She looked around as if she wanted to make sure no one saw her — and then she took a bite.

Then she saw Adam coming.

"Oh, Adam—this is so good. Here, have a bite," she said quickly.

Adam took a bite, too. Soon both Adam and Eve began to act very strangely. Eve never even called, "Here, Kitty, Kitty," and patted me. They didn't stop to wait for God to come and walk with them. They always did that every evening. Instead, they looked at each other in such an odd way. I saw them pull some huge leaves off of the fig tree. Then they ran behind a big bush.

God came looking for them. I heard Him call, "Adam!—Where are you?"

"We're over here, God, behind this bush. We didn't have any clothes on, so we made some coverings out of big leaves, and then we hid. We were ashamed."

"Who said you were naked?" God asked. "Did you eat some of the fruit I told you not to eat?"

Then Adam spoke up quickly. "Eve here—this woman You gave me—gave me some of the fruit and I ate it." After all, he didn't *have* to take it, just because Eve held it out to him. Did he?

"Why would you do a thing like that, Eve?" asked God.

"The Snake persuaded me to do it," said Eve.

God was very angry with the Snake. "You will never be a handsome animal any more. After this, you must crawl on the ground, instead of standing up tall and slim and beautiful. Ever after this, people won't like you. Some day I will send Someone to crush your head but you will hurt His heel."

But God didn't stop with the Snake. The man and the woman must be punished, too, because they didn't obey God. "Eve, you will have pain when your children are born. Your husband will rule over you." Then He turned to Adam. "You will have to work hard to earn your food. Thorns and weeds will make your work harder."

Then God said something that made me very sad. "You have to leave the garden, before you get a chance to eat the fruit of the tree of life and live forever." And He sent them away.

I miss Eve. Why would anybody have to eat forbidden fruit, when she had lots of other good fruit? But speaking of food, I must go see if I can find a nice fat mouse.

Scripture: Genesis 3

The Tiger's Floating Prison

Noah and the Ark

The first time I heard that awful pounding racket I was prowling around in the valley. I jumped from rock to rock and half-slid down a rocky slope. The pounding was louder and louder. I stood very still for a while before I padded softly in the direction of the noise.

A person was pounding on wood—on a big dark object made of wood.

A big man with red hair came up and asked, "What are you doing, Noah? You are making an awful racket."

"I am making an ark because God told me to."

"What for?"

"God said it is going to rain. We will need a place to go to be safe."

And then I saw that man start to laugh and laugh. "Oh, Noah, you are funny! You don't believe that, do you? We have never had rain here. You are wasting your time." And he laughed again. Soon he had gathered a whole group of men and they all laughed and pointed at Noah.

Noah kept on pounding.

Then he said, "You will see. When God says it is going to rain I believe it is going to rain. And when God says for me to build an ark so that those who go inside will be safe from the flood, I am going to obey God. If you want to be safe you can come into the ark."

"Who, me?" asked the red-headed man. "I will never go into your ark. You are foolish."

We heard Noah pounding day after day, day after day, for a long, long time. Then one day it was quiet. I was padding along that day, when Noah touched my head. I saw that my girl-cousin was walking along with Noah, so I followed, too.

I saw zebras, and elephants, and giraffes and rabbits and squirrels and—just every animal you could name. We walked along two by two right toward that ark. Then up ahead I saw the zebras step on a board and walk right up inside it. So all the rest of us did the same thing.

Inside the building was plenty of space for even the elephants and giraffes. And hay and grain and fruit and nuts. Nobody seemed to be going anywhere else, so I finally curled up in a corner and slept.

When I woke up, it was night inside the ark and something was hitting it on top. "It is raining, Noah," I heard his wife say. "Just listen—the water is really coming down."

Then I heard a faint voice from outside the ark. "Noah, Noah, let us in. We were wrong. We didn't believe God."

It sounded like the voice of the red-headed man.

But Noah couldn't open the door for God had shut it.

The noise of something gently hitting the roof of that building bothered me at first, but I finally got used to it and hardly noticed. About that time, something else happened that scared the wits out of me. The building began to move. It rocked back and forth. I felt funny when I tried to walk. My cousin stood there, waving her striped tail back and forth with the rocking motion. We both finally got used to the rocking, too.

Cousin and I had a new fun-game and the elephants didn't seem to mind. We jumped from one elephant to the other, and down to the hippopotamus and back up to the elephants. It was like playing on the rocks at home. The elephants just batted their trunks at us and dropped hay on us.

One day I noticed the noise outside on the roof had stopped. The barking and meowing and honking and quacking and crowing and growling still went on, but it was quiet on the roof. We hardly noticed the back and forth rocking of the ark. Before many days we felt a slight bump, and the ark was still.

I can't tell you how long we were in that prison. First Noah let out some birds. I wished I could fly. But soon one of the birds came back. Later he let out another bird, but it never came back. And then finally I saw the door open. Cousin and I jumped to the earth. It was squishy but still it was earth. There were rocks, too. But they were not the rocks I used to climb on. I didn't see that red-headed man anywhere.

At least we were out of that prison. Cousin and I could see the parade still coming down out of the ark. Then Noah and seven other people came out, too. They were safe in the ark, and all of us animals had been safe in the ark, too. Everything that God said really happened! When Noah believed God he knew what he was doing.

Scripture: Genesis 6—8

Mortimer the Mouse Sees Joseph's Capture

Joseph Is Sold

There were so many sheep in my field one day, that I was almost afraid to get out of my hole and run around — I might get stepped on. Or, worse yet, I might get caught in a mouthful of grass and become a sheep's dinner! And besides, there were ever so many men taking care of all those sheep. My favorite hole was close to their tent.

All the men were walking around, looking after the sheep, when suddenly they began to talk very loud. "Look over there, Levi—there comes our brother!" one shouted to another.

"Oh, Judah," another man yelled, "there comes Joseph!"

"There comes the dreamer," said another.

A young man kept walking toward them from across the field. The men kept talking. "I don't like Joseph. He said God gave him some dreams, and that someday we will bow down to him. He thinks he is really something."

"Let's get rid of him," said another brother. "Then we shall see what shall become of those fancy dreams."

"Yes, let's kill him. We don't want to have him rule over us."

Then a big man said, "No—let's not kill him. Let's just throw him into a deep pit so he can't get out."

That is what they did. When the man got close to them, two of them took hold of his shoulders and dragged him along to a deep hole. They took off the pretty coat he was wearing and tossed it on the ground. I almost got covered up, for I was nearby.

"Reuben! Reuben! Help me!" Joseph shouted from down in that pit.

But nobody came to help him. It sounded like he was crying down there in that deep hole. But the men just went off and started to eat their lunch.

"Now we'll see what becomes of his dreams!" one said.

"Yes," said another, "he won't be around, so we can't bow down to him. He talked like we'd all be his servants some day!"

"Well, we've put an end to that talk!" snorted a short, fat man.

Then they saw a lot of men and animals coming toward them. They were big animals—bigger than sheep. Their necks were long and they had humps on their backs.

"I've got a good idea!" one of Joseph's brothers said. "There's a caravan. Those men are going to Egypt. Let's sell Joseph to them."

"That's a good plan," said Judah. "If we sell him, he will end up as a slave in Egypt. We'll be rid of him, but we won't be guilty of killing him."

Somehow they got Joseph out of that deep hole. The men with the funny big animals took Joseph along with them and put pieces of shiny coins in the hand of one brother.

The biggest brother came back from where he had taken his sheep. He saw that Joseph was not in the hole any more.

"Where is he?" Reuben asked the other brothers.

"See those traders going, way over there?" answered Judah. "Well, we sold Joseph to them, and he will be a slave in Egypt."

The men picked up Joseph's pretty coat. I saw them kill a baby goat.

"Now, let's dip the coat in the goat's blood," one said. "We'll tell our father that a wild animal must have killed Joseph. Those dreams of his just aren't going to come to pass. We will see to that."

Of course I knew what really happened. But, after all, what could I do? Who would listen to a mouse? (Mortimer the Mouse exits.)

Mortimer the Mouse knew part of the story. But he didn't know that Joseph actually became a slave in Egypt. Worse than that Joseph was thrown into prison. Someone said he did something that he never did. But God got him out of prison and made him next to the king.

His brothers came to Egypt to buy food when they didn't have any in their own country. They had to get Joseph's permission. They bowed low before him. So Joseph's dreams came true because God gave them to him.

Scripture: Genesis 37—45

Freddie the Frog Watches Baby Moses

The Baby in the Bulrushes

A little boy kept trying to catch me the other day. I was just hopping about in my home in the bulrushes, and he came down to the edge of the water and saw me. Now, the Nile River is a great big river—much too far across for me to jump. But along its banks, tall reeds are growing. They make a nice hiding place, if anyone wants to play hide-and-seek. And I played hide-and-seek with that little boy.

"Aaron!" I heard his mother calling him. She called just in time, too—he was about to catch me. I made sure I hid where reeds were thick and grass grew near. My green skin makes me hard to see in that place. I could watch that boy and his mother and big sister from where I sat. They had their arms full of reeds.

"This is a good place—right here," said the mother. All of a sudden she was standing too close to me for comfort. But I kept very still. If I jumped, they would hear me. When she spoke, the boy and girl came nearer to my hiding place, too.

"We are going to take these reeds and make a little boat for baby brother," Mother explained. "It will be like the big boats that sail on the Nile River—only it will be little, like a basket. It will be just right to hold our baby."

"It will leak—won't it, Mama?" asked the girl.

"No, Miriam," answered Mother. "We will stick the reeds together with pitch, just as men do when they build a sailboat. When we get the basket-boat made, we will put it in the water right here."

"Why do we have to put our baby in the water, Mama?" asked the boy.

"Because the king's soldiers might get him if we don't do that, Aaron," said his mother. "The king doesn't want us Hebrew people to have any baby boys. So he sends his soldiers out to find if there are new baby boys in our homes. But I am not afraid of the king or his soldiers, for God is going to take care of our dear little baby."

The three of them went away. The sun went down, and the moon

54

came out and made the water sparkly. The next thing I knew, it was sunny and warm again, and I heard the same three people talking.

"We will put the basket into the water," said the mother as she waded into the edge of the river. "Baby brother is sleeping now and his little boat will float and gently rock him. Aaron, you come with me for I must help your father in his work. Miriam, you hide behind those reeds and watch the little basket. We want to know what happens to our baby."

"Will we see our baby again?" asked Aaron.

"Oh, yes. Your daddy and I have asked God again and again to watch over our dear little baby boy. I know God is going to take care of him." Then she took the little boy by the hand and walked away.

I saw Miriam, the girl, kneel down behind some reeds—so close to me that I could have jumped on her!

Then I saw a fancy lady coming down to the river. It was the princess! The king's daughter! Another lady waved a palm branch over the head of the princess. Maybe the breeze from the palm branch kept the princess cool. If I get warm, I jump into the water. And—wait a minute! That's just what the princess did too. She took off some of her pretty clothes and waded into the water. Then she saw the basket boat.

"Bring me that basket floating in the water," said the princess to the other lady. The way she spoke, that lady had to be a servant.

"Yes, your highness," answered the servant lady. And she walked right out into the water and picked up the basket. I heard a funny noise. The baby was crying.

"Open it quick!" said the excited princess.

The trembling maid set the basket down on the shore and unfastened the cover. Then I heard both women exclaim, "Oh! Isn't he sweet!"

"He must be a Hebrew baby," said the princess. "He is so fine and healthy, we must try to take care of him."

Just then the reeds near her moved, and out stepped the baby's sister.

"Shall I find a nurse for the baby for you?" asked Miriam.

"Oh, would you, please!" said the princess. "I was wondering where to get one."

Miriam wasn't gone very long before she came back down to the water—with her own mother—the baby's mother!

"Will you take care of this child for me?" asked the princess.

"Yes, I can do that," said the mother quietly. She never let on for a minute that she ever saw that baby before.

"I will pay you wages for your work," said the princess. "You may take him to your home. We will name him Moses because I drew him up out of the water."

"Hurry, Miriam," said the mother. "We must tell your daddy that God has saved our dear baby boy."

The princess and the servant lady finished bathing and started back to the palace. They were talking about the cute baby boy who would come to live at the palace some day, when he got big enough.

It's a good thing they couldn't understand frog language. Because I really croaked right out loud in a great big frog laugh. It was the father of that princess who was making soldiers kill the Hebrew baby boys. His own daughter had just saved the life of one Hebrew baby boy, little Moses!

Scripture: Exodus 1; 2

The Cow That Walked Between
Walls of Water

Crossing the Red Sea

You just never in this world would believe some of the adventures I've lived through—but let me tell you about them anyhow. These things don't happen in the everyday life of any old cow, but all these events happened because I belonged to a herd of a family in Egypt. I heard my master say that Moses had gone before the king to ask him to let his slaves, the Hebrew people, go free. He said Moses told the king, "If you don't let my people go, God will turn the water in the river into blood."

I didn't believe it until I went down to the river to get a drink of water. It was blood! If you think that is bad, you should have been there when the flies were so thick it looked as if my hide was black velvet covered with sequins. Maybe that's what caused all the boils I had later—or maybe it was the lice. But maybe the God who caused the water to turn to blood was bringing all those horrible things so the king would let God's people go free.

One day it got so pitch dark I couldn't see the horns of the cow standing right next to me. We stumbled around, bumping into everything. On another day hail pelted down on us. It really hurt. I was standing in a field, not far from the border of a different farm. I could see the cows in the next field grazing peacefully. Not a bit of hail was over there! While everybody was worrying about the hail, I jumped over into the field of that Hebrew family where there was no hail.

It seemed I would not get to enjoy the quiet field very long. A few nights later some men drove all the cattle together and we all trotted along pretty fast for awhile. I never saw so many cattle together in one place—and sheep—and donkeys—and camels! All were trotting along. Behind us, men and women were running and shouting and singing. Some children were crying for their mothers.

We finally stopped to rest—because we couldn't go any farther. I saw mountains on each side of us, and in front of us was a lot of water. "We've come to the Red Sea," said a man. "How will we get across?"

I was ready to rest. Why not stay where we were for awhile? But those men were shouting, "The Egyptians are coming! They'll kill us all!"

A tall, strong man with a stick in his hand stood up on a little hill. Some men yelled at him, "Why did you bring us here to die, Moses?"

He answered, "Stand still and watch God save you."

Then I saw this Hebrew man, Moses, walk right up to the edge of the water. He held the stick out in front of him. He stayed there a long, long time. Then all the animals and people started to walk. We walked right into what had been water in front of us—only the water wasn't there. It was piled up high on each side of us. I saw it out of the corner of my eye. But I didn't spend any time looking. I was too anxious to get past it.

At last we had all climbed safely up on hard, dry ground, and the people were singing and shouting again. Then a man screamed, "Look! The Egyptians are coming! Look at all the horses and chariots and soldiers! They are coming through the bottom of the Red Sea just like we did!"

Then Moses stood beside the piled-up water. He held out that stick again, and those waters swooshed right down on top of all those horses and chariots and soldiers. All of them were drowned.

Now we are all following a cloud that moves ahead of us in the daytime. At night the cloud is all red, like fire. Wherever we go, I am surely glad I got out of Egypt. My new masters have Somebody special taking care of all of us.

Scripture: Exodus 14

The Donkey That Really Talked

Balaam and His Donkey

Everybody knows about make-believe mules that talk. But I really *did* talk—and I mean I talked people-talk, not donkey-talk. What happened to me was enough to make any donkey talk!

Balaam, my master, was famous because he could prophesy. God told him what was going to happen, and he told people what God said. We lived near the Euphrates River. The Euphrates River flowed through the garden of Eden.

One day we had company. I heard the men say that King Balak had sent them. One of the king's messengers said, "A great many Hebrew people called the people of Israel are camped in our country. I am afraid of them. They won a battle over some enemies that had conquered us. They will surely wipe us out if we have to fight them."

"What can I do about it?" asked my master Balaam.

"King Balak wants you to come and curse the Israelites," said the messengers. "We know that when you curse someone he is cursed and when you bless someone he is blessed."

"Stay here overnight," my master invited the men. "I will ask the Lord what He wants me to do."

In the morning, I heard Balaam tell the men he would not go with them. "God told me those people are blessed, so I cannot come and curse them."

The men went away. But after awhile more of the same kind of men came again.

"We have nice presents to offer you from King Balak," said the men. "If you will come along and curse Israel for us, you will have great honor from the king."

My master looked at the nice gifts. He told the men, "If Balak gave me his house full of silver and gold, I could not do something God told me not to do. But stay here overnight while I talk to God about it."

Now, that was a silly thing to do. He had talked to God before, and God had already told him no. But Balaam really wanted those nice presents, so he talked to God again. This time God said, "Go on with them. But don't say anything except what I tell you to say."

In the morning, my master, Balaam, put a saddle on my back. Two of his servants saddled up their donkeys. We started down the road, following the strange men. All at once, right in the road, I saw the angel of the Lord, and he had a sword in his hand! Believe me, I got out of that road, fast! My master thought I was being stubborn, and he hit me with his hand and made me get back on the road.

We hadn't gone very far when we came to a narrow road between two vineyards. There was a wall on each side—and right in the middle stood the angel again! I moved as far over as I could to go around him. When I leaned against the wall, I hurt my master's foot. Now, he was really angry. He hit me harder than before and shouted at me.

I carefully went on. Soon, there stood the angel again. This time, there was no way to get around him at all. I just fell down in front of him. Balaam began to beat me with his staff. That's when I began to talk.

"Why are you beating me?" I asked him—and I was talking people talk! "You have beaten me three times."

He was very angry. "If I had a sword right now, I'd kill you!" he said.

"Haven't I always carried you faithfully ever since you first got me?" I asked. "Did I ever behave this way before?"

"No," my master, Balaam, admitted. And just then, he saw why I behaved so strangely. He saw the angel of the Lord, standing there holding that sword in his hand. Now it was Balaam who fell down before him. He must have realized that it was the Lord God, Himself!

"Why did you beat your poor donkey?" asked the Lord. "I stood in your way, because you insisted on disobeying Me. If your donkey had not turned aside, I would have killed you."

"I'll go back home, if You say so," said Balaam.

But the Lord told him, "Go with the men, but say only what I tell you to say."

It turned out to be an awful waste of time. Balaam could not please King Balak at all, because the Lord only let him bless Israel. He wanted all those lovely presents, but he never got them after all. The people of Israel were God's people. As long as they obeyed Him, God took care of them and blessed them.

Scripture: Numbers 22; 23

The Camel Watches the Battle

Gideon's Three Hundred

I guess you might say I owe my life to a snake. A viper bit me. Why it picked on me, I'll never know. But of course God meant for it to be, because it spared my life. There were thousands of us camels in the Midianite army the day I got bitten. We had galloped along for many miles.

"We are going to the land of Israel, to wipe out all the poeple," said one man to my master. "Yes," said my master, "that's where we went last year to burn up all their food and all their crops."

I was there last year, too. I felt sorry for those people. After we burned up their food, we stole their sheep and their goats and their cows.

Then my master said, "Some of them think that their God can help them. But we know He can't. We have thousands and thousands of camels and soldiers. And they have only a few people. I've heard they are so scared they are hiding in caves. What could their God do?"

My master said, "I heard one of their men cry out, 'O God, help us! Save us from the Midianites.' " Then he laughed. "Their God can't do that. We Midianites are too strong!"

We stopped for awhile, and that's when my accident happened. That viper bit me on my left foreleg, and my leg swelled up, right where it bends, until I couldn't walk, much less run. My master got disgusted and told me, "You can just stay here. I'll ride one of the extra camels." So off he went.

Not that I minded. Without him along to keep me moving, I could hobble as slowly as I wished to. Who wants to have a man on his back all the time? A camel can't even stop and grab a mouthful of thorns, no matter how many thorn trees he sees! So I just took my time. Hundreds and hundreds and hundreds of camels kept going past me, until finally all I could see was the dust they left behind. I kept hobbling toward that dust.

My leg finally quit hurting. I tried kneeling, and it didn't hurt quite so much when I bent it. The hot sand felt good on it. I got to my feet after awhile, and I was able to walk faster. By the next day, I could gallop along on my sandshoes. I rushed in the direction of the dust.

Lucky for me the other camels had stopped. I saw them up ahead. At least I thought it was lucky. But I really wasn't anxious to let any man ride me, so I slowed down. No use running into trouble if I could help it.

Water. Somewhere near all those thousands of camels, there was water. I walked carefully around the edge of the herd of camels and men. At last I came to a river and I drank and drank. Some other camels were doing the same. It's a wonder there was any water left.

There were some people on a hill, not far from the herd I was with. I saw them walking around. They might come down to get a camel. I'd better be careful.

I wandered away from the herd, munching happily on some thistles and thorns. You wouldn't like them, but I do. I saw that most of the camels stayed right where they were. The men were there to tie them so they couldn't walk away, or I know they would have been looking for bushes to eat. It was getting dark, and I was looking for a good place to rest, when I heard such a loud noise, over on that hill where I'd seen men walking.

Suddenly those people on the hill were shouting—they must be the Israelite people! It seemed they were all around the camp of the Midianite soldiers. Crash! Crash! What was that? Then flames of fire spurted up toward the sky. They were all around our camp. I saw our Midianite soldiers jump up and start to kill each other. Some of them started to run away. And the soldiers of Israel chased them. And Israel won that battle. Did their God help them? They didn't have many soldiers but they won the battle.

The last I saw, the camels were still running. I think I'll wait till things quiet down before I go home.

Scripture: Judges 6; 7

The Fox, the Lion and the Strong Man

Samson

My name isn't "Foxy" for nothing. It wasn't just luck that helped me escape the day that awful giant of a man caught 300 of my relatives. But let me tell you about that man first, and how I got to know him.

I was curled up on my bed of leaves behind a big rock in a grape arbor one morning about daylight. An arbor is a kind of orchard where there are a lot of grape vines. I was catching a snooze after a busy night of chasing mice for my supper. My bushy tail was wrapped around me like a fuzzy blanket. Then I heard this person stomping along the path near my bed.

Somebody else heard him, too. I was wondering whether to keep very quiet or get up and run 25 miles an hour to a safer place, when I heard a roar! A young lion landed on the shoulders of that big man as he stomped along the trail. He should have known us animals would hear him coming.

I thought I had seen the last of that man. He wouldn't disturb my sleep anymore. I felt sure the lion would take care of him. It was nothing unusual for a lion to kill a man if he attacked. But this one lost the fight. That man just took his huge hands and tore that lion from one end to the other. He left the cat and went on his way. He didn't bother me.

The news got around in the hill country. Some of my relatives heard that the man's name was Samson. They said he often visited his country's enemies in Timnath because he had a girl friend there. I saw him again later on. The bones of the lion were near the path. I had seen bees flying near it. He saw them too.

"Hm—honey," he muttered. He stooped down and got some of the sweet stuff on his fingers and licked it off. He mumbled something about a riddle for the men of Timnath. "Out of the eater came forth food and out of the strong came forth sweetness." He took some of that honeycomb and went on, eating as he went.

I don't know what really happened next — I only know what I

went through. It was the worst day in the history of us foxes in that valley. One of my cousins told me it all started when Samson went to see his wife in Timnath and found out she was somebody else's wife by then. Oh! You'd never guess what a terrible thing he did—and we hadn't done a thing to hurt him. Samson went out and caught 300 of us foxes—don't ask me how. He must have had a lot of dogs and a lot of slaves to help him. I only know that when I heard my relatives yipping and I saw him coming, I ran into a hollow in an olive tree and stayed quiet and out of sight. I heard him chasing foxes right past my hiding place.

You'd never believe what happened next. Nobody could be that mean—but Samson was. He took those 300 foxes and tied every two of them together by their tails. He put a blazing piece of wood between the tails and turned them loose in his enemies' territory. Well, naturally the foxes ran as fast as they could go, trying to get away from that fire. They ran through the deep grain and it caught fire. They ran through the grape arbors and vines caught fire. Even olive trees were blazing. Some of the foxes did get away after the fire burned the vines that fastened their tails together. Their tails were never pretty and bushy anymore, but at least they were alive.

We heard more about Samson after that. Once he killed 1,000 men in my country with nothing but a bone. Some Philistines locked him in a city one night and they planned to kill him. He got away by pulling the gates right up out of the ground and walking off with them.

We were glad to hear that the men in our country finally did capture Samson. I heard they put out his eyes and made him work like a mule. I went to a big celebration. The Philistines, Samson's enemies, were offering sacrifices to Dagon, their fish-god, because they thought he gave Samson to them. I know better. Samson's God was the same as mine. My God made everything, and he can do anything. He let Samson get punished for the bad things he did.

I was trotting along to hide and to watch the celebration over Samson's capture when I saw and heard the great crowd. I never saw so many people. They were standing around shouting and teasing Samson. All at once Samson gave a great push on those pillars that held up the house. They broke, and the whole temple fell down, and all those people with it. I saw the roof come crashing down on top of a man who was under it—that man was Samson. He won't bother any more foxes.

Scripture: Judges 13—16

Curly the Sheep

The Boy David Takes Care of the Sheep

Sheep may all look alike to you, but David, my shepherd, didn't think so. He chose me for his special pet, and it's easy to see why. When I was just a lamb, I got caught in a thornbush. My legs were scratched and bleeding, and I got one nasty cut on the head, too. David took good care of me as soon as he found me. He rubbed some warm, smooth oil on the cuts.

After that, he kept me close to where he was, until I was all well. If I even looked as if I wanted to jump across a ditch to get some greener grass, he reached out that long stick of his and pulled me back toward him. Naturally, I got to know him better than some of my cousins who did not walk so close to him. He saw what a pretty wool coat I had—whiter and curlier than that of any other, I was sure. David must have thought so, too, because he called me "Curly." After a time, he did not even need to reach out for me with that stick—he just called out, "Curly!" and I trotted over to him. David thought each one of us sheep was important. He loved us and took good care of us.

Whenever we stop to rest in the afternoon, I like to lie down near David and listen to the songs he sings while he plays his harp. He sings "The Lord is my shepherd: I shall not want." He loves to sing about his Shepherd. When I listen to what he sings I think that the Lord must be a Shepherd about like my David. He takes good care of His sheep. He even puts oil on David's cuts the way David does on mine. David thinks his Shepherd is very important and he talks to Him a lot. I hear him often. David loves Him too, because I hear him say that he wants to please his Shepherd.

We had a thrilling adventure one day. We had just finished getting a drink of water in a little quiet brook, when an old ewe let out a loud "Baa-a-a!" I saw David look at her quickly and I saw the same thing he saw: a lion had a lamb in his mouth—the ewe's little lamb. No wonder that mother cried! I didn't follow David, but he really moved fast. In nothing flat he surprised the lion as it tried to run through the flock carrying the lamb in its mouth. David grabbed that lion and held onto the mane with one hand and beat the lion on the head with his club. That was the end of the lion.

Another time, a bear tried to make off with a lamb. Like a flash, David was after it and he rescued that lamb, too.

Twice in the summertime we were trotting along after David as he was leading us to a good pasture. I saw a nice bunch of grass and started toward it. All of a sudden, that hooked stick of David's caught my hind leg and I nearly turned a flip. When I looked around I saw a big snake wiggle in behind some rocks. One of my cousins who was far away from David was bitten on the leg by a snake, and she died.

David was with us every day. I always felt safe, knowing he was watching out for snakes and bears and lions. Life was peaceful and pleasant, for we could rest each day and hear David play on his harp.

One day, a stranger came out to the field where we were. I heard him call, "David!" David shouted back, "Come over here!" I was standing near David when the two young men were talking.

"Your father sent me for you," said the stranger. "The prophet Samuel is at your father's house. He is asking for you."

"Me?" asked David. He was surprised. "What does he want?"

"You go to the house and find out, and I will stay here with the sheep until you get back."

I said "Baa-a-a" to David as he ran off to his father's house. It was late in the afternoon when he came back. He was very quiet. He looked up into the sky and talked to the Lord after the stranger went away.

Not long after that, another shepherd came out to take care of us. David patted my head and said, "Goodby, Curly. I have to go and play on my harp for the king. And what do you know, Curly? Some day I am going to be the king. God has said so. Isn't that wonderful?"

My Shepherd boy is going to be the king! Maybe it is because he loved us sheep and took such good care of us. Maybe, too, it is because he loved his Shepherd and really tried to please Him.

Scripture: I Samuel 16; Psalm 23

The Rabbit That Missed the Stew

David and Goliath

Home was such a happy place when I was young. My mother and my seven brothers and sisters and I live in a valley between two hills, not very far from the Mediterranean Sea. Sea gulls flapped over our hole occasionally. But something happened to change all that.

Men came—they were soldiers. There were more men than there were rabbits in the whole valley. First, a lot of men came and stayed on top of one of the hills. Before long, many more men came and stayed on top of the other hill. We didn't feel safe, with so many of our enemies on both sides of us.

We weren't safe, either. Rabbits began to disappear. I was hiding behind a rock one day and I saw one soldier carry off my cousin by his hind legs. The man was saying something about "a good stew." Whatever stew is, that's where the rabbits were going. Since they didn't come back, I decided I didn't want to land in any stew. So I made myself scarce.

Of course, I had to come out of my hole and go down to the brook for a drink of water once in awhile—and that's when I saw *him!* Now, I have seen a lot of men on these hills, wearing heavy armor and waving their shiny swords. But this man—wow! He was as big as two men put together!

That monster shook the ground as he came too near my hiding place by the brook. Then he roared out, "Send a man to fight with me!" Huh! The big bully! Why didn't he pick on somebody his own size!

This roaring went on for days. There never was a fight. I can see why.

Then on another day I went for a drink down at the brook. I saw a small man scarcely bigger than a boy who had a staff in his hand. I heard the men call him David. He stooped down to pick up some stones out of the brook. Then he started running right for the huge monster.

67

The monster laughed. "Do you think I'm a dog? Do you think you can fight me with a stick?"

Then David said to the monster, "You come to me with a sword, and with a spear . . . but I come to you in the name of the Lord of Hosts . . . ." Then he put one of those stones into a sling. He whirled his arm around and around and then I saw that stone fly out of the sling. It landed right in the giant's forehead—it hit so hard it went in and didn't even come out. Then I saw David rush over to where he fell. He took the monster's big sword, and hit him under the chin with it—and his head fell right off!

Believe me, I was glad. I was shaking so hard I was dancing a jig down there by the brook. I almost fainted from fright when I saw what happened next. All the men on one hill were running down the far side of the hill. The men on the other hill—the one David came from—rushed down right toward me. I thought my time had come! But they didn't even see me. They were chasing the other men. Many were shouting, "Hurrah for David! Hurrah for David!"

They kept right on running past me, trying to catch the men from the other hill. I hope they caught them and put them in their stew. With all of them gone, our valley may be a happy place again.

Scripture: I Samuel 17

Butler, the Raven, and His Free Air Delivery

Elijah and the Ravens

Don't you think I'm handsome, with my black dress suit? That's why some boys started calling me "Butler." I have to stay dressed up, because that's the only outfit God gave me. If you don't think I'm beautiful, let me remind you that we can't have everything. Actually, my reputation leans more toward brains than beauty.

Usually, I eat whatever is handy—and so do my relatives. My cousins at the North Pole like dead seals or fish. In South America they will settle for tigers—dead ones, of course. In England they even eat fruit, as well as small animals and worms.

I fly for a long distance with my strong wings, watching a flock of sheep. If I see a lamb that just hobbles along behind the flock, something tells me it is sick. When it falls down dead, I swoop down and start helping the farmer. Nobody wants a dead lamb around. Some of my friends join me for breakfast and really clean up the carcass.

Ravens have been around a long time. Did you know that my great-grandfather was the first living thing to leave Noah's ark after the Flood? Noah let him out of the window when he thought the trees might be above water. Grandpa didn't see anything but water, so he kept on flying around. He had strong wings, and he was as big as I am—24 inches from his beak to his tail. That's a pretty big bird. At least I think I'm pretty — so black I look purple and shiny.

God gave me an important job to do one day. And that's how I got my name in His book about Elijah. This man Elijah was a prophet. God told Elijah what the people needed to know and then Elijah told the people what God had said. One day I swooped down on a dead lamb just in time to hear Elijah say, "There won't be any rain for three years unless I say so." Now, anybody knows that grass and trees and vines need rain. Soon there would not be anything green for animals to eat. I had an idea there would be lots of food for us ravens, though, when animals started falling over for lack of food. We ravens would have no problem, for we would have water as long as there were rivers.

God told Elijah to camp beside a brook named Cherith and hide there where the king couldn't find him. The king might command Elijah to pray for rain. But where would Elijah get food out there by the brook?

"You're going to take it to him," said the Lord.

"Who, me?" I asked.

"Yes. You and some of your relatives are so clever I know you can get away with it. Here's what I want you to do: Every day when the king's servants start carrying his food to him in those baskets on their heads, you and your friends just dive down and get a chunk of meat and a loaf of bread and flap away from there as fast as you can. Fly right to Cherith and drop the food down by Elijah."

It was an interesting game while it lasted. Every morning and every evening we waited around in some olive trees near the palace. When the servants came along with the food, we flew around and grabbed some and made off with it. Oh, they got mad all right. Some threw rocks at us, but God saw to it that none of us were hit. We were serving Him, and He took care of us.

But the game ended. You see, with no rain in the land, Elijah's brook went dry. God just told us one day, "You won't need to snatch any more food for Elijah. I have moved him to another hiding place, where someone else is feeding him. Thank you for taking care of my prophet."

"We were glad to do it," we croaked as we flew away. In fact, we had so much fun we grabbed a few meals for ourselves now and then. Nobody can say we don't have an exciting life.

Scripture: I Kings 17

70

Job's Favorite Camel

Job and His Troubles

I am a camel — you guessed that, didn't you? I'm not just *any* old camel—I am one of 3,000 camels that belonged to a rich man named Job. Well, actually, I can't say whether he was rich because he owned us, or whether he owned us because he was rich. Anyhow, we lived a good life in Uz, near the land of Edom.

At least my life was what I called "good." Servants took care that all of us camels had all we wanted to eat. Bushes and brambles and thorns were plentiful. No, the thorns didn't bother me. The bristles around my mouth are there for a good reason. Besides, I *like* thorns. Don't you?

While we're talking about *me*, I feel sure I have something handy that you don't have. But then, you wouldn't need it. I have eye-shades—like window shades, only these pull down over my eyes. I can still see, but the shades keep out sand that blows from the desert I live near.

Of course, my life isn't all just eating and sleeping. Sometimes a servant of Job comes and puts something soft and warm on top of my hump. On top of that he piles a piece of animal skin, and then he covers it all with a woolly sheepskin. This is strapped on under my belly. When my master travels anywhere over the sands he rides on my back, on top of all those skins.

I can't honestly say I am proud to carry the rich man on my back—or anybody else, for that matter. But I guess I am better off than some other animals. The donkeys carry big skin bags full of wool. The bags weigh more than Job does. The servant makes me kneel, and then I sit down on my hind quarters. I feel like getting up when Job starts to climb on my back. When he puts one leg over the seat on my hump, I want to raise up and let him fall off head first, but that servant has a sharp stick to remind me not to move.

That stick didn't stop me from grumbling, though. I turned my head clear around and looked Job right in the eye and put on a mournful expression. But he was not at all sorry to take me away from pleasant hours of grazing. It didn't bother him when I made it quite clear that I didn't want him on my back.

Job was never mean to me, though. I guess I can be thankful for that. Some of my cousins had scars from the beatings they get from their masters. Especially poor Sheba. One day a servant put one of those high seats on Sheba's hump and climbed on, and she would not move. He beat her with his rod—hard!—till I saw red streaks on her flanks. Another servant found out why Sheba was so stubborn. She had hidden her new little colt and nobody knew she had one. She would not leave it behind.

The little people at Job's house often came running and shouting out to where I was. It seems to me that Job kept more and more of those little people, the longer I lived. In fact, I counted seven of them. At first they took turns getting on my back and riding. I could hardly feel the weight, but I turned my head clear around and looked them in the face and whimpered, and I made sure to grumble all the time they rode. But don't think that stopped them! When the little people grew bigger, each of them got on a different camel and had races. I don't like to brag—but guess who won! That's why Job chose me.

I had been Job's camel for about twenty years when *trouble* came. Before that awful time, I hardly knew what trouble was, but I surely found out. It all began on a beautiful spring day. The ground was soft from the winter rains, and the oxen were plowing the fields so Job's servants could plant grain. Some of the animals were peacefully nibbling the green grass the rains had brought. Personally, I was finishing off some bramble bushes. I heard men shouting and oxen lowing and running in a herd, with men on horses behind them. Later on, I heard what happened.

A servant ran panting to my master's house and fell at his feet. "A band of robbers took all the oxen and donkeys. They killed all the servants except me. I hid in a cave till dark."

My master had not finished telling his wife about that before another servant came running up. He fell down at the door, panting. "All the sheep and shepherds are burned up—except me." That meant 7,000 sheep. That must have been some awful fire. But that wasn't all that happened. I was lucky Job was riding me as he went to his son's house to tell him about the robbers and the fire. Because if he had not been riding me, I might have been stolen, along with the 3,000 camels that the Chaldeans came and herded away.

Now it looked a little foolish to me, but my master, Job, did not stand and wring his hands like the servant did. He did not shake his fist and ask, "Why did this happen to me?" He just bowed his head to the ground and I heard him say something that sounded like "Blessed be the name of the Lord." If it had been me that lost so much, that's not what I would have said. I even grumble when everything goes fine.

Job wasn't a rich man any more. His animals were gone. But he still had his family and a comfortable place to live. And he still had me. But before he could turn around, Job had lost his family, too. All those little people that grew up were having a feast at the home of the oldest one, and the house fell down on them and they were killed.

Next thing I knew, Job wasn't riding me anywhere. I saw him one day, standing on a pile of ashes. At least, I guessed it was Job, because his wife said, "Job, why don't you curse God and die?" Otherwise, I wouldn't have known him. He had these awful-looking sores all over him. I'm glad he couldn't ride me—I might have caught whatever he had.

This went on for quite awhile—Job staying out there, sick. Some men came and talked to him. I heard him talking to Somebody I couldn't see. After a long time—at least it seemed that way—Job went to his house.

Strangest thing happened. Before long, Job was richer than he used to be. As far as I could see in every direction, there were animals. There were twice as many of us camels as there used to be—twice as many of everything, except the little people. But soon there were just as many of them as there used to be.

Job still talks to Somebody I can't see—sometimes even when he is riding along on me. I wonder if that is the One who gave him all those animals.

Scripture: Job 1; 2; 42

73

A Lion with Lockjaw

Daniel in the Lions' Den

Do you have any idea what it's like to be down in a dark cave all the time, locked in? I can't even get out to find me a nice rabbit for a feast. My wife and I and some of my cousins and other relatives should feel honored, I guess. We're the king's lions. That makes us important. But we're like any other lions: we like to hunt for our food when we get hungry. Down in the cave, we have to wait until King Darius' servants decide to throw down something for us to eat. It hardly ever hits the floor before we gobble it up. We don't even stop to play with it, as your cat plays with a mouse.

One day I was standing on all fours, eyeing the door of the cave, trying to figure out how I could get outside, when I heard some men talking right by the door.

"This is the king's lion cave," said one man. "Be careful you don't fall through that door."

"That gives me a good idea," said the other man. "You know this fellow, Daniel, the one that prays to his God every day? The king likes him so much we'll never get anywhere with him around."

"Yes, I've been thinking about him, too."

"Well, why don't we get the king to make a law that nobody can pray to anybody but him, for thirty days? If anyone does, he'll be thrown down into this den of lions."

That sounded like a good idea. I didn't know this Daniel, but he might make a good meal—for a few of us, anyhow.

"Let's go," said the other man. "King Darius will think it's a great idea. He's proud of himself, you know."

I heard their footsteps as they walked away. I wondered how long it would be, before Daniel was tossed down to us. We soon got the idea it would not be very long. Somebody else walked up to our door, and stood there awhile. Then I heard feet walking back and forth. From what the man kept saying, I knew it must be King Darius himself.

"Why did I ever make such a silly law?" the man asked, right out loud. If he was asking me, I wished I could tell him, "So we lions can have a good square meal." But he didn't ask me. He just went on talking to himself out there. "There is just no way I can get out of giving the order for Daniel to be thrown to those hungry lions. Daniel—my faithful prince. He does more for me than all those other princes who just want to be popular in the palace. I have to do what the law says, so Daniel must go to the lions. He's always talking about the God he prays to. Maybe that God can do something to help."

I licked my chops. It would take a mighty strong God to do anything for Daniel, once he came through that door.

We stood up on all fours when we heard a lot of footsteps close to our door. Now was the time. The door opened, and a man with his hands tied behind him was standing there. All at once I felt so sleepy—not hungry at all. I went to the farthest corner of the cave and curled up. I noticed that my wife and all the other lions just lay down and went to sleep. I tried to open my mouth to snarl a little, but it wouldn't even open.

The man landed on his feet so close to me I could have grabbed his ankle without moving. But I was just too tired to bother—and besides, like I said, my mouth wouldn't open. Something mighty funny was going on. Maybe that God the king talked about had something to do with it.

Daniel must have decided my heavy mane would be a nice soft pillow. First thing I knew he laid his head on me and went to sleep.

I heard feet walking back and forth all night up there, whenever I happened to wake up. Some light was beginning to show around the edge of the stone in the doorway when I heard the stone move. The king shouted down to this man Daniel: "O Daniel, was your God able to help you?"

"Oh, yes," Daniel answered as he got up from my nice soft mane and climbed out of our cave to join the king. "God sent His angel and shut the lions' mouths."

So that's what happened. An angel. That's why I couldn't open my mouth. The king gasped and then he started to blubber. Even so I could tell he was happy. But he soon began giving orders I was happy to hear.

"Get those men who caused me to make that law," shouted the king. "Throw all of them and their whole families down to the lions."

Food at last. Who wants Daniel when he can have a whole family?

Scripture: Daniel 6

The Fish That Caught a Man

Jonah

Hello, there! Did you ever go fishing? Did you ever catch anything? If you did, you took it home and somebody cooked it so you could eat it. You swallowed that fish, didn't you? Well, I want to tell you here and now, here's one fish that swallowed a man—a man that wasn't even salted.

I wasn't really looking for a man to swallow, even though men had swallowed some of my cousins. I was swimming along, minding my own business, when all at once the water began to churn. I shot up to see what was happening on top, and a big wave pushed me around. Wow! It was rough up there.

Somebody else was up there. Something dark was riding up and down on the waves. I wondered what it was. I swam around below it, where the water wasn't so rough. Just then, something made me open my mouth wide, and I swallowed some water. But something big washed down with it, and something hard hit the sides of my stomach. Surely that wasn't a fish—it wasn't slippery.

I never swallowed any fish that felt like that did inside me. Sometimes it did not move at all, but I could feel some vibrations that made me know it was still alive. Now, I like for my food to do me some good — not just stay alive inside of me. I swam as fast as I could, and turned over and over, thinking I would surely get that *thing* so dizzy it would curl up and die.

It didn't. I really felt sick. My stomach hurt, and I couldn't eat. After three days of this I was fed up. I shot up to the top of the water when I saw we were getting close to land. I wiggled my way until my whole head was on the sand, and then my poor stomach turned wrongside out. And out came that *thing!* It was a man, one of those *people* that had swallowed my cousins.

He was still alive. I saw him stand up and start running away from me as fast as he could go. But Somebody said something, and he stopped.

"Jonah!" said the Voice.

"Yes, Lord?"

"Go to Nineveh, that big wicked city, and tell them I am going to wipe them out."

"Yes, Lord. This time when You tell me to go to Nineveh and tell the people to stop being so wicked, I will really go. I won't run away as I did the last time. Being in that fish really taught me a lesson." And Jonah started to run.

It was time for me to get back in the water. I scooted backwards, and swished around and shot away from the shore. I didn't want some man to swallow *me*.

I hope Jonah got to Nineveh and stayed there. I never want to take him for a ride again.

Scripture: The book of Jonah

The Eavesdropping Owl

The Story of Nicodemus

You know how it is with us owls. We have to make our living at night, because we happen to like little animals that run around in the dark—such as mice.

One night I was sitting in an olive tree, not far from Jerusalem, looking around for a good dinner to come my way, when I saw a Man. He was just sitting there on the ground, leaning against another olive tree. Somehow, I wasn't afraid of Him, so I stayed in my tree and just asked him, "Who—o—o?"

I found out Who in just a little while. Another man came along, walking so quietly I could hardly hear him. He stopped beside the Man and said, "Rabbi, I know you are a teacher from God." So that's who He was—a teacher from God.

The Man just said, "Except a man be born again, he cannot see the kingdom of God."

I didn't know what He was talking about. It was all just noise to me. I knew I came out of a shell, and I could never in all the world find a shell big enough to get back inside of to start over! And anyhow, I wasn't a man. But I saw no mice to chase right then, so I shut one eye and listened. An owl can learn a lot just listening, instead of making noise all the time like a mockingbird.

That other man didn't seem to know what the Teacher was talking about. He couldn't figure out how to start life over, any more than I could. The Teacher said something about being "born of water and of the Spirit." Then He said very clearly — and I heard every word— "Ye must be born again."

In the next breath, the Teacher started talking about the wind. Now, I knew what He was talking about. Sometimes the wind blows so hard it puffs dust over my feathers until I look like a common chicken, instead of a handsome owl.

The Teacher said, "Nobody can tell where the wind comes from or where it is going."

That other stupid man didn't seem to know what He meant at all.

Any wise owl knows you can't see the wind at all, but you can sure see the dust it brings!

The Teacher said, "How can I teach you anything about heaven, when you don't even understand what happens on earth?"

But He went on, anyhow, telling the man some things about God. I know God is the One who made me. And He made the little mice I like to eat, too. The Teacher told the man that "God so loved the world, that he gave his only begotten Son, that whosoever believeth in him should not perish, but have everlasting life."

The man didn't say much, while the Teacher was talking. He just listened. Maybe he wondered where he could find God's Son, so he could believe in Him. He'd better, because the Teacher said it was very important.

He said, "He that believeth on him is not condemned." But it didn't sound too good for anybody that didn't believe. From what the Teacher said, that unbeliever was "condemned already." I don't know what "condemned" means, but it didn't sound like a nice word.

I wished I knew where I could find God's Son, too—I'd believe in a hurry. Specially since that Teacher went on to say something about people that like darkness instead of light. They were bad, because they did bad things in the dark. But after all, He wasn't talking about owls.

Scripture: John 3

Porky the Pig

The Prodigal Son

You have no idea what fun it is being a pig. Nothing to do all day long but eat and sleep. My brothers and sisters and I get pretty and fat. Lately I've noticed there aren't as many brothers as there used to be. Nobody seems to know where they went. But it's no use for me to worry, as long as people keep giving me lots of corn to eat—and anything else nobody wants.

Let me tell you about the funny man that came to feed us our corn and husks. His clothes were different from my other master. For one thing, they weren't at all pretty. And naturally, they got dirty as he took care of us pigs. We love to roll in the mud, and we brushed against him with our muddy backs.

But the way he looked wasn't the funniest part of this man. It was the way he sat around and talked to himself. He thought I was sound asleep, but I was just lying there in the mud with my eyes shut, so I heard what he said.

"Taking care of pigs!" It sounded to me like the man actually snorted like I do. "What an awful job for a rich Jew's son!"

A rich man's son? My old master had nicer clothes. And besides, what's wrong with taking care of pigs? I'm very fond of pigs myself.

"I've wasted all the money my father gave me," the man said. "Now I have nothing left—not even friends." He went on muttering about his friends. "They never were friends. They just wanted me to buy fun for them with my money. When my money was gone, so were they! How foolish I have been."

People must be something like pigs, if the man's talk is true. We pigs believe in "Every pig for himself." If I see a nice juicy vegetable peeling that my little brother is about to get, I put my snout down there and shove him out of the way and take it for myself. But that's the way my brother treats me, too.

"Why, oh, why did I leave my father's house?" the man moaned. "I am so hungry! I almost wish I could eat some of the trash I've been feeding these pigs."

Now, wouldn't he be a funny sight, down on the ground next to me? He'd never be able to eat that corn before I could grab it!

The man still went on talking to himself. "There's so much food in my father's house. Even the servants have more to eat than they need." I raised up and pricked up my ears. That might be a good place to go — if I knew how to get there.

I saw him just sitting there, staring at the sky. "I know what I'll do," he said, "I'll just go back home and I'll tell my father I want to be one of his servants. I'll say, 'I did wrong and I'm not worth being called your son. Let me be a servant.' "

Well, what do you think the man did? He got up from the ground and began to walk away from us pigs as fast as he could go. I started to follow him down the road, but somebody came shouting out of the house. It was the man who used to take care of us. He threw a rock at me and said, "Go on back to your pen!"

I wish I knew where the funny man went. I was always a good pig. He might have been glad to give me a home where he had all that food. He never came back, so I guess they fed him well.

Scripture: Luke 15:11-20

Shorty, the Donkey, Leads the Parade

The Triumphal Entry

Let me tell you about the day I got broken to ride. I behaved so nicely that—well, you never saw anything like the way people fussed over me. Believe me, not every donkey colt carries its first rider as well as I did mine.

My adventure really began early one morning, when two men came and led me to a hilltop. I could look down the hill and see a city wall and houses, and one big pretty building nicer than all the others.

Nobody had ever been on my back before. When someone tried to ride my brother, he kicked up his heels high in the air, and that man went flying over his head. I thought that was a good idea. I didn't want to carry anyone around. If people thought my brother was wild they should see what I would do!

The two men led me to a Man with kind, gentle eyes. "Here is the little donkey, Jesus," said one of them. Jesus patted my face. He was so kind I would have done anything for Him. Then the men put their cloaks on my back. I'd seen my mother with something on her back. I suppose it was to be expected. The clothes were not heavy, so I didn't mind. Then Jesus got on my back. He touched my head softly and spoke to me kindly. "We're going to Jerusalem," He said. I wasn't afraid of Him at all. He let me know I was to walk down the hill to the wall, so I started walking.

You never saw so many people. They seemed to come from everywhere! Men and women and boys and girls. Some were waving palm branches in the air and shouting, "Hosanna to the Son of David!" Was that the Man on my back? It wasn't *my* name. Nobody ever called me anything but Shorty, because I wasn't fully grown yet.

People seemed to think the road wasn't good enough for me to walk on. Men and women spread their cloaks on the road. Some of them threw down the palm branches they were waving. Others tossed flowers for me to trample on.

I really felt honored. Never had a donkey been treated so well. This praise and kindness lasted all the way to the wall. We went through the gate of the wall and started down the road toward that big pretty building I saw. Then the Man got off my back.

Little children ran along beside Him, singing praises. Gruff voices came from big men standing near that pretty building. "Make those children keep quiet!"

Jesus walked along toward the building, and I was left standing. The children kept following Him and singing. I felt a little foolish by then. You see, it finally dawned on me that all the singing and shouting was for Jesus—not for me! Even after He got off my back, the crowd of people followed Him and kept shouting.

When the gruff voices complained again, Jesus said, "If these people were silent, even the stones would cry out."

"Blessed is He that comes in the name of the Lord!" someone shouted.

I felt a little bit sad. Jesus was so kind and gentle. I'd like to have Him for my master all the time. Maybe if I waited, He would come back.

That's why I was still there some minutes later. Jesus went into that big pretty building. Someone called it the Temple. Many of those shouters went inside, too. Pretty soon I saw something very strange.

Sheep and cows came trotting out of the Temple. Right behind them, some men rushed out, making angry noises and waving their arms wildly.

Then I saw the kind, gentle man, Jesus, standing there at the entrance. He did not look kind or gentle just then. He had a whip. "You have made my Father's House a den of thieves!" He shouted. The last I saw them, those mean-sounding men were still running.

Somebody finally led me away to my home. I kept looking for the Man to come back and ride me, but He never did. I wonder why.

Scripture: Matthew 21

Doolittle the Dog

The Crucifixion

The way things turned out, it was a good thing I slept all day. That's how I got my name, Doolittle. My master tossed me some breadcrusts and a bone for supper and then he got ready to go somewhere. Of course I followed him. There might be an adventure more exciting than barking at everything that came near the house.

Many people's feet and robes brushed against me as I trotted behind my master down the brick streets. It was quite dark in the narrow space between buildings, and above the shoulders of the walking people, I could see the blaze of torches now and then. The feet were hurrying along, all going in the same direction. It hurt my ears to hear all the loud talking and shouting.

The feet stopped in a place where there was more space. I followed my master as he went to stand near some mumbling, shouting men. Big men in bright, fancy robes swished through the crowd. They stopped to talk to men here and there. One stopped by my master's side and said. "The Man is trying to destroy the faith of our fathers. He must die. Let's all shout, 'Crucify Him!' "

Then a voice came from up in the air somewhere. I looked up and saw a man on a porch high up in a building. He was pointing to a Man near him as he talked. This other Man looked familiar to me. All at once I realized He was the One I saw riding a donkey into the city, just a few days before that. People went wild, throwing down clothes on the road and shouting "Hosanna!" But that night He had a different robe on, and there were ugly thorns on His head, and blood trickled down His face. He just stood there, sadly looking at us down below.

The other man yelled down to the mob: "You always free a prisoner at this time in your feast. Shall I turn loose this Man you see here?"

"No! No!" shouted many voices. "Let Barabbas go free!" I didn't see Barabbas.

The man on the porch said, "What shall I do with Jesus?" That must be the poor Man with the thorns.

Then I heard loud screaming. "Crucify Him! Crucify Him!" That's what those other fancy men were talking about. They sounded so mean I leaned over against my master's legs.

After the screaming stopped, the man on the porch stood up and washed his hands in a basin of water, right in front of everybody. I couldn't tell you why. By that time I was thirsty and I wished I could get at that water.

Then my master started walking again, and so did all those shuffling feet. Their loud voices kept saying, "He ought to die." Nobody said why.

Suddenly everybody stopped talking. My master was pushing his way through the crowd to find out why, so I followed him. That's when I saw that poor, quiet Man with the thorns on His head. He was on His knees under two huge pieces of wood. He couldn't stand up. Finally, some soldiers put the wood—it was a cross—on a strong, dark-looking man. This man began to walk, carrying Jesus' cross. Soldiers walked next to Jesus.

The crowd kept on walking and walking, right out of the city gate and to the top of a hill. There the soldiers lay the cross down on the ground. They yanked Jesus over to the cross. I didn't like the way they jerked Him around and I said so. But they didn't pay any attention to my barking. They went right on doing something so awful I hate to tell you about it. I'll whisper it: They pounded nails right through His hands and feet and fastened Him to that cross.

One soldier said, "Lift up the cross!" Someone helped him stand it up. They set the bottom of it down into a hole, so it stood up in the air with Jesus still on it.

Two other men were put on crosses, too, and they screamed and cursed the soldiers. But Jesus didn't. My master stayed there awhile, and once I heard Jesus say, "Father, forgive them; they know not what they are doing." I rather thought the soldiers did know, but maybe He was talking about the mob.

My master sat down on the ground, and I stretched out for a snooze. I don't know how long I slept, but I woke up when the ground under me began to shake. I looked around for my master and he was already halfway down the hill. I saw him by a flash of lightning. It was pitch dark and I almost got stepped on trying to catch up with him.

At the bottom of the hill, my master turned around and stood still. He looked back up the hill. I looked, too. I saw three crosses standing up. Jesus was on the one in the middle.

My master said sadly, "Why did they do it? Jesus never did anything bad in His life!"

I didn't even wag my tail. It wasn't a time to be happy. I liked that Man with the thorns on His head. And mean men had done something awful to Him.

Scripture: Matthew 27

The Ox That Wore a Wreath of Flowers

Paul at Lystra

My name is Ollie the ox. I had a happy childhood. You can see that I grew up strong and well. That's because I was well fed. When I was almost as big as my mother, I was brought to live in a fancy place.

"This is the temple of Jupiter," my master said as we came near to it. Of course I didn't answer him back. He couldn't understand my language. I just said, "Ma-a-a!"

Once in a while I walked about in the courtyard. On a pile of stones in there sometimes I saw fire blazing. After that, I noticed another of my ox friends was missing when I came outside to walk around. Part of the time I stayed in a pen and enjoyed the hay brought to me.

One day I heard a big commotion outside my stall. Many voices were talking somewhere nearby. Then one voice said loudly, "Stand up on your feet!" Maybe there was a fight going on out there.

The noise outside grew louder than ever. Such shouting and singing. A young man rushed into the temple and exclaimed to the priest, "Get an ox ready to sacrifice! The gods have come down in person!"

"How do you know?" asked the priest.

"They spoke and that crippled man who never walked before, just stood up and began to jump around."

"I'll bring the oxen for the sacrifice," said the priest.

Sacrifice? That was what the priests talked about when they took my ox friends out by the pile of rocks. And then my friends never came back. I never saw them again. I decided I didn't want to be a sacrifice.

Soon a priest came to me with a wreath of flowers in his hand. He patted my head and put the flowers around my neck. Then I started to tremble. That was what the priest had done for my ox friends when they became sacrifices.

"Hail, Jupiter! Hail, Mercury!" Such a racket! I wanted to run back to my stall, but the priest had a firm grip on that rope around my neck. I wasn't going anywhere.

Then we heard one loud voice. "You must not make a sacrifice to us!" he said. "We are not gods. My name is Paul and this is my friend Barnabas!"

"But only gods can make a helpless man walk," someone said.

"Hail to the gods!" shouted the crowd again.

The priest tugged on my rope. I began to get the picture: he was pulling me closer to that pile of rocks! I pulled back, and so did my ox friend close by. He had on a wreath of flowers, too.

Then Paul and Barnabas began to talk about a God that was greater than Jupiter. "The God we serve is the One who made the heaven and the earth and the sea. He made everything else, too. He sends the rain and helps our crops to grow so we will have good food. We don't want you to make a sacrifice to us for we are not gods."

The priest quit pulling on my rope. The people just stared, they were so surprised. Then they shuffled off in different directions. The priest led me back to my stall. I heaved a sigh of relief. Paul had saved my life.

Scripture: Acts 14

The Jail Rat, Songs and Salvation

Paul and Silas

A rat gets around to a lot of interesting places — and you'll have to admit I've had my share of adventures. Especially after I tell you what happened one night in Philippi.

I was scurrying around on the dirt floor of the jail, looking for a few more crumbs some prisoner might have dropped. Men's feet got in my way—I had to climb over quite a few of them. Some prisoners made loud noises at me when my tail tickled their feet.

The light from a torch suddenly lit up the blackness, and I scampered for a corner. I would have had to run past that torch to get to my hole. So I just squeezed into that corner and hoped nobody would see me.

The jailer and some guards were bringing some new prisoners. Now, I've seen a lot of new prisoners brought in. They usually have to be dragged along, while they shout curses at the jailer. They scream while they are being chained and fastened in the stocks.

The stocks must be awful. The prisoner's feet and arms are put into some holes in wood, and they just sit that way. They can't lie down and curl up for a nap like I can. No wonder I hear them groaning and cursing.

But these new prisoners were different. Their bare backs looked just as sore as those of other prisoners. They were fastened into the stocks. But they were not cursing and shouting at the guards.

"What have they done?" I heard one prisoner ask another.

"Those are the Jews who were going around talking about Somebody named Jesus," said the other. "Just before I got caught stealing, I saw that little man there—Paul, they called him—I saw him cast a demon out of a girl fortune-teller."

"Why would a man get put in jail for doing good?"

"The girl's masters were mad—they couldn't make any more money from fortunes. So they caused trouble for this Paul and his friend Silas."

So the new prisoners were named Paul and Silas. After the torch had gone out of the jail, I crept over to where they were.

"Praise the Lord, Silas," I heard Paul say. "Jesus let us suffer for Him."

"Lord Jesus, give us grace to behave like Christians should. Our backs hurt, and we are so uncomfortable, but You are near."

They were talking to this Jesus. And then I heard the strangest commotion. Those two—Paul and Silas—began to sing. Now, I've heard a lot of noises in jail. But this is the first time prisoners have done any singing. Everything was quiet in the other cells. The other prisoners were wondering what kind of men could possibly be happy in jail.

And then it happened. The old dirt floor began to shake. I ran around in circles, wondering where I should hide. Such a racket. I decided to get outside, and fast! Not a minute too soon, either. From behind a rock, I heard such a roaring, and men shouting. Suddenly the doors to that jail just flew open. Nobody touched them—they just opened. Wow!

Here came the man with the torch. He had his sword in his hand. As he passed by my rock, he was saying, "All the prisoners have surely escaped, and the rulers will kill me because they got away. I'll kill myself first."

But before he could do anything so awful, I heard the voice of Paul. "Don't hurt yourself! We are all here!"

The jailer ran to where Paul and Silas were quietly standing. They were free from the chains and stocks, but they did not run away. "What must I do to be saved?" that jailer begged them.

"Believe on the Lord Jesus Christ and you will be saved," both Paul and Silas said quickly.

The jailer said, "I believe in Jesus. I'll tell Him right now." After that, he was a different man. He locked the other prisoners back up, but he took Paul and Silas to his home and fixed up their hurting backs. I sneaked along behind to see what was happening.

I'm glad I did. The jailer's wife fixed dinner, right in the middle of the night. And when they got through eating—guess who cleaned up the crumbs!

Scripture: Acts 16

The Galley Rat Sails on a Ship

Paul's Shipwreck

Have you ever sailed on the sea in a big ship? I have—lots of times.
A ship is a favorite home for my brothers and uncles and cousins
and a lot of other relatives—and, of course, for me. No, it's not
because we need the fresh air of a voyage. In fact, we spend most of
our time below deck, where the fresh air doesn't reach.

I will tell you why we especially liked the boat from Alexandria—
the one where we had our big adventure. On that boat, there was
more than enough wheat to go around. Each of us rats had a sack to
himself. The trick was to rip out just a thread or two at the corner, so
a few grains of wheat would trickle out—not enough so those giants
up on deck would see the hole and say, "Rats are in this wheat. We
must poison them." Ugh!

This voyage started out about like any other. You expect a boat to
rock back and forth. This one did. We could hear people talking. One
man was ordering others around. We heard feet scurrying on deck.
People make so much noise when they run. They should learn how to
run as softly as I do.

We were enjoying a pleasant feast, when we heard water sloshing
against the boat. The bags of wheat heaved from one side of the
storeroom to the other. I almost got my tail caught between two
sacks as I dashed out of their way. But if I thought that was a close
call, it was nothing compared to what came next.

While the ship tossed around like a box, I heard that loud-voiced
man say, "Put a rope around the boat, to hold the boards together." I
could feel the boat go up, up, up. When it came down again, there was
such a crashing and groaning, we all hid behind the wheat bags and
rolled our eyes. We didn't want to be drowned rats!

Some of those men almost got us the next day. They came into the
storeroom and carried out some of the wheat. I heard one say,
"Throw it overboard." They never brought the wheat back, so I
guess it all went into the water. There were a few bags left, and we
still had something to eat. Of course, we could always find leftovers

in the cook's galley.

But we soon found out the cook wasn't doing much cooking, and nobody was doing any eating. Those men up there running around were scared! They kept saying, "Shipwreck! There's going to be a shipwreck!" I hid behind some ropes and listened to them talk. After all, I was bound to share whatever happened to them. I saw one man who wasn't a sailor; he was smaller than the others and not too good-looking. This man made a speech.

"Nobody is going to lose his life in this storm," said the man.

"How do you know that, Paul?" somebody asked him.

"An angel of God told me tonight. He said, 'Fear not, Paul, you are going to appear before Caesar and God will save the life of everybody on the ship.' "

I hoped that meant us rats, too. Does God take care of rats? Oh, you already know the answer to that. If He didn't, I wouldn't be here telling you about it!

Paul said something else I wasn't too happy about. "You will be cast on an island." I wondered what he meant by that. I found out soon enough.

The men came in and carried out the rest of our wheat. It was hard to find food enough to keep us going. We found a few grains in a corner, and some on the stairs where the sack had leaked. Paul's next speech was good news to my ears.

"All of us must have something to eat, so we will be strong enough for the hardships to follow." He ate some food himself, to show them he thought it was important. Then the others began to eat. From my hiding place I saw crumbs drop on the deck. I could hardly wait to clean them up. A ship must be kept neat, you know. It is no small job to clean up crumbs after 276 people. I heard somebody say that's how many were on this ship.

The big adventure happened when daylight came. I heard that loud man order the boat steered to some land he could see near. But the wind kept blowing and the boat didn't go where he said. It got stuck. The waves kept crashing and crashing around us. I thought any minute I would be a goner. People were running and screaming, "I can't swim!" Somebody shouted, "Get a board and ride it to shore!"

That's what I did. Some of my cousins decided to stay with the part of the boat that was stuck. I'm glad I made it to shore on a board that broke off the ship.

On dry land, I scrambled for cover under a brush pile. And none too soon. That man Paul stooped over right near where I was hiding and gathered up an armful of the brush. He carried it to the fire. Seems there were people on the dry land, and they started this fire to help the wet people dry their clothes and get warm. Anyhow, something wiggled out of the brush in Paul's arms and I saw it dangling from his hand.

"It's a poison snake," I heard a soldier say.

"Paul is going to die," said a sailor.

But nothing happened to Paul. The snake fell into the fire, and Paul went on and ate his food as though nothing had happened.

I found a nice warm house not far from there and prowled around looking for food and a place to sleep. Somebody in there was groaning. The next day men came in there, bringing that man Paul. He seemed to be following me around.

Paul talked to Somebody I couldn't see. "Lord, please make this man well, in Jesus' name." The groaning man got up from his bed and smiled and thanked Paul.

After that, all the sick people came to see Paul to get him to make them well. You never saw so many sick people. When they came they were sick, but when they went away they were well.

I got along fine on that island. For three months there was plenty to eat and fine hiding places. But all good things come to an end. One day I heard people shouting and running. "A ship is landing here!" they were saying.

"We are going to Rome," Paul said.

While everybody was busy putting food on the new ship, I made a leap for the deck and disappeared quicker than a wink. Life was so exciting around Paul, I decided to go right along to Rome and find out what happened next!

Scripture: Acts 27; 28.

Resources for Puppets

You Can Be a Puppeteer, by Carolyn London. Moody Press, 820 N. LaSalle St., Chicago, IL 60610.

Childcraft Encyclopedia. Almost any library.

Visual Aid Encyclopedia, Eleanor Doan. Regal Press, Glendale, CA 91209

Bible Puppet Plays, Ewart A. and Lola M. Autry. Baker Book House, 1019 Wealthy St., Grand Rapids, MI 49506.

Puppets and Bible Plays, Bracher. Fortress Press, 2900 Queen Lane, Philadelphia, PA 19129.

Tom Tichenor's Puppets, Abingdon Press, 201 8th Ave., S., Nashville, TN 37203. Detailed help by one of television's first puppeteers.

Remo Bufano's Book of Puppetry. Macmillan Company, New York, NY 10022. Check the public library.

Teaching with Puppets, Bruce Rodrick. Standard Publishing, 8121 Hamilton Ave., Cincinnati, OH 45231. Suggestions and directions for making and using puppets in Bible teaching.

Charlie Churchmouse, Violet Hodson. Standard Publishing (above). 35 story scripts with finger puppet patterns.

Puppets Help Teach, Diane Warner. Accent Books, P.O. Box 15337, Denver, CO 80215. How to use puppets, and puppet dialogues on many Bible subjects and for special days.

Aha! I'm a Puppet, by Avis Reid. 205 W. 16 St., Glencoe, MN 55336. Fifty ideas.

Teaching Bible Stories More Effectively with Puppets, Roland Sylvester. Concordia Publishing House, 3558 S. Jefferson Ave., St. Louis, MO 53118. Good ideas.

Higley Publishing Corporation, P.O. Box 2470, Jacksonville, FL 32203. Write for price list and information. Large assortment of ready-made puppets, including eight large ones.

Contemporary Drama Service, Box 457, Downers Grove, IL 60515. Write for information about puppet kits which have plays and patterns for puppets.

Puppet Pals, 100 Belhaven, Los Gatos, CA 95030. Puppet kits and complete instruction kits. Range in price from $1.00 to $6.95. Quality at minimum cost. Write for price list.

The Puppetry Store, 3500 Tyler, N.E., Minneapolis, MN 55418. Books and pamphlets about puppetry, including patterns and plays.

Balda Art Service, Oshkosh, WI 54901. Object lesson books adaptable for puppet talks.

Paula's Puppet Parade, 10005 E. 41st St., Tulsa, OK 74145. Puppets of people, cartoon characters, birds, a monster. $8.00 up. Self-addressed envelope for list.

Puppet Ministries, 10156 East 22nd Place, Tulsa, OK 74129. Puppets, tapes, patterns, skits, stages. Puppet seminars conducted.

Dale and Liz VonSeggen, 58250 Benham, Elkhart, IN 46544. Puppets for sale ranging to stage-size for performances (even 30 inches tall). Also scripts for plays.

Puppets, Puppets, P.O. Box 2128, Dallas, TX 75221. Scripts, puppets, kits, tapes.

Sheram Puppet Industries, P.O. Box 1402, Columbus, OH 43216. Wide variety of puppets and prices. Request catalog.

Maher Ventriloquist Studios, Box 420, Littleton, CO 80120. Attractive hand puppets, as well as dummies and scripts.

Fellowship of Christian Puppeteers Newsletter, Pineview Community Church, P.O. Box 5404, Albany, NY 12205. Small subscription price. Patterns and scripts. News of puppeteers in churches throughout the land.

Goodwill Store, Salvation Army Store, Thrift Stores and Garage Sales. Source of used stuffed animals.